God's blessi... (handwritten inscription)

EATING MY WORDS

One Woman's Spiritual Journey

Virginia Stiles

PublishAmerica
Baltimore

First printing

At the specific preference of the author, PublishAmerica allowed this work to remain exactly as the author intended, verbatim, without editorial input.

ISBN: 1-4241-1826-3
PUBLISHED BY PUBLISHAMERICA, LLLP
www.publishamerica.com
Baltimore

Printed in the United States of America

DEDICATION

It is with deepest thanks that I dedicate this book to the townspeople of Arcadia, Westside and Vail, who know exactly the pride of living in one of Iowa's small towns. Also to my sister and brother-in-law, Heinie and Judith Boomgarden for always being there for me. And to Janine Kock who understands what it really means to offer support to a friend. To Rev. Keith Weiland and Gordon Greta for their constant, but gentle, nudging. And, of course, to all those who have gone on ahead of me to the promised land, particularly my mother, Pauline, and my friend, Evie.

INTRODUCTION

This is a simple story. It is a personal story. It is a story of my own faith journey in what we call life.

I have been a writer for over 40 years, and in all the years I worked as a journalist I told the stories of many, many people. But I have never attempted once to tell THIS story.

Over the years I have shared many of my family's stories through my weekly column in the newspaper, or in specially prepared sermons spoken from the pulpit. In all those years, some members of my family have questioned my memory in relating some of the details of the story, though most of their questions were always asked with a great amount of love.

In recalling these events, it is not my intention to dispute any facts, or to get caught up in details, or to be malicious or offensive in any of these stories, but simply to relate my own experiences and feelings. And how I believe God played a part in one woman's life.

Thanks to my family for their encouragement particularly to my sister and brother-in-law who stayed by me through many days and nights of struggling with the aftermath of a stroke, and to all the wonderful people of Westside for being a beacon in the night and sticking with their pastor through some of her darkest days. They have been a wonderful reflection of God's Word in the world. They are a blessing.

This is my story. And God's.

CHAPTER ONE

For as long as I can remember, I have had but one dream. To be a writer.

Whether it is with newspapers, magazines or television made no difference to me. I just knew that journalism was for me. Even though it wasn't known as "journalism" then.

But it wasn't supposed to be like this.

It was a job that was supposed to be one which gave me some income until something better came along.

From the earliest memories of my childhood, I would watch what was happening in the neighborhood, compile all my notes and then develop a "neighborhood" newspaper.

You have to understand that the town in which I was raised had a population of about 864 tops, at its peak. Called Scranton, in later years it was always necessary to explain that it is a town in Iowa, not in Pennsylvania. It truly is a community where everyone knew what everyone else is doing. We had a weekly newspaper in our town, but the neighborhood grapevine was the best source of news around.

It was a typical Midwestern town, consisting entirely of a population of Caucasians who had little or no idea what racial prejudice amounted to. There were one or two really poor families who lived in that part of town where we were rarely permitted to go as children. There were a few families in the town who were considered wealthy. There were definite classifications of poor, poorer and poorest.

We were probably in the "poorer" category, since our mother once had to briefly submit herself to accepting welfare payments shortly after the death of our father. She was, however, so humiliated by having to accept charity that she was determined to get a full-time job—and was successful.

I'll never forget that night. It was a dark, cloudless night when our grandparents brought the news that our father had died in Chicago of what was believed to be a self-inflected drug overdose. It was on April 24, 1953. He was 34 years of age. In what people thought was the prime of his life. Family members preferred to call the cause of death a "heart attack," but his death was actually self-induced, if truth be known. He was an over-the-road truck driver, specializing in delivering livestock. While my mother worked in retail stores prior to their marriage, she had little thought her career would be anything other than as a homemaker. My mother actually got past his death and all the turmoil that preceded that event in her life fairly well, though not without times of pure loneliness. Although she had opportunities to re-marry, she never would. I was nine years old at the time of my father's death. It was hard to know what "forgiveness" was supposed to mean, especially when my Mom had been so very unhappy.

At first she used her skills to earn a few dollars for food—taking in washings and ironings for other people, and doing some clothing alterations. With two girls—ages 9 and 10—as well as fighting the loss of self-esteem by being on welfare, she knew she had to do something.

Friends suggested she might get a job as a teller in the local bank and, though she was not sure she could do it, she took a chance. She was especially encouraged because she had been employed by the owner of the bank, who lived in Coon Rapids, when she had been a young girl. She was very optimistic.

We were delighted when they called to tell us she was hired. Her paycheck was a whopping $130 per month and we were suddenly elevated to the "poor" class. She was able to secure this job, so she was told, because she could type—an experimental class she took as a high school senior in 1932. She used to tell us that the school board was hesitant about starting that class, because it was believed to be too difficult for high school students. That now seems unbelievable in a time when we are teaching keyboarding to elementary students.

I remember that once the bills were paid, one of the first "luxury" items she purchased was a pair of matching lamps for our living room. They cost all of $5 each.

It was a true status symbol. We had "arrived."

My sister and I were part of the first "latch key" generation, but we didn't know it. Doors were never locked, but we spent a great deal of time on our own while our mother worked. We were told that, in order for her to be able to work full time, it would be necessary for us to help around the house. We did that because we wanted to help. However, it left little time for being just kids.

In my "leisure time" I would fantasize along with the movie news reporters about breaking the big story or uncovering a tremendous scandal which would reveal political corruption and save the future of democracy for the world.

No doubt about it, the reporter portrayed in the movies was

glamorous and adventuresome—not to mention courageous, especially when it came to protecting the First Amendment rights. It was the early 1950s, and reporters were still a respected lot.

If reporting didn't work out, perhaps I could write the Great American Novel. Others had tried, but I would do it. The plot was just swimming around in my head someplace.

There were other dreams as well, but not as vivid. I wanted to join the Navy, but the military did not have the prestige it carries today. It was generally thought of as the place kids went who couldn't do anything else. I put that on the bottom of the list. I dreamed about radio news broadcasting. I really think I could have handled that eventually. And I dreamed about being a preacher, but knew it was an impossible dream for girls. It was a profession open only to boys. In my last year in high school I became extremely interested in speech, especially original oratory, so that cultivated an interest in broadcasting. But when radio turned into television, I think I always knew my looks would never permit me to be successful there. I might have lost weight to be skinny enough for the job, but, in my mind, the mirror told the real story. I was not considered overly attractive. I could live with "pleasant."

Our "neighborhood" newspaper, which contained a great deal of vital information, such as who had company over the weekend and who was having the ladies' afternoon bridge group—along with news in other parts of the community, such as the school—sold for a nickel. We had purchased a used typewriter for my sister and I to use while in high school and that's how our neighborhood newspaper was "printed." It became so popular the other kids in the neighborhood wanted to contribute articles for it. We grossed about $1 per week, which paid for the paper. No reporters were ever paid. We did it for the glory of seeing our names in print.

Nothing more.

As time went on, our activities in school kept us too busy to keep the neighborhood publication in operation. So, it gradually disappeared from the scene. But I became active in the high school newspaper, which was published only three times a year, and was printed on a mimeograph. What it lacked in quantity, it made up for in quality. I still think some of my most creative efforts were published in that newspaper.

There were no dreams of going to college. There was no money. College educations were for those who wanted to be teachers or scientists or doctors or lawyers. Not journalists.

When I graduated from high school, I knew I was ready for the "big time." I started filing applications with the daily newspapers in the area. I didn't care where I started; I was ready to try anything just to be employed by a newspaper. I even applied one time for a position as a classified ad clerk. That was desperation, believe me.

After about five months of searching for that special journalism job, it became apparent I could not live off my mother much longer, no matter how much disgusting housecleaning I did. Oh, I did things to supplement my income, such as type term papers for high school kids and for college students—for a price. In those days I was pretty fair with the keyboard. Time does change things.

Anyway, Christmas was approaching and I had very little money with which to purchase any presents. Not that this was any different than other years, but I had dreamed to be earning my own way to the top of the journalistic ladder by this time. I was starting to look at the "help wanted" ads in the local and nearby community newspapers—for anything that would pay.

I finally convinced myself that I would have to settle for

something—anything—to provide my share of money towards the family income.

It appeared as though my dreams would have to wait.

In a neighboring community, an industry was hiring. But the problem was complicated by the fact that our family owned no car. At that time, it wasn't really necessary to have a car, except if you wanted to go to the county seat for business at the courthouse. Even our small town had a doctor, not to mention a grocery store, variety store, hardware store, a movie theatre and all the things one considered to be the necessities of life.

Of course, there was no furniture store, but the variety store and hardware included small appliances and small furniture items. Going out of town to shop was a real treat, and one saved for just such an occasion.

When we wanted to visit out of town relatives, we took the bus. We did the same for business calls, unless a neighbor was going and invited us to tag along. As I said, my mother was particular about accepting anything which appeared to be classified as charity.

As I contemplated seeking a job at a factory in that nearby community, I knew there were others in town who worked there, and for a fee, I knew I could ride with them to the job site.

So, with somewhat of a downcast spirit, I began preparing my resume to send to those industries.

At the local coffee shop and ice cream parlor—I said we had all the necessities in this small town—one could hear all the latest news about who was doing what, who was traveling and what business was in trouble. It was on a trip to that coffee shop with my mother one day that I learned the local weekly newspaper was being sold.

Well, it was hardly what I had envisioned for the beginning of my journalistic career, but it might be a job. The publication was being purchased by a newspaper in another town, and they were looking for someone to manage the office.

I went right down to the office and let it be known I was available.

That day I was hired. It was a Thursday.

I began my work on Friday, January 13, 1961. I have always felt it was my lucky day.

There was no doubt in my mind that this was the beginning of what I envisioned to be a long and lucrative career in journalism.

My job description? Well, it was to answer the telephone, sweep the floors, make a few calls for news items for what was then referred to as the "society" page, and generally keep the place open for business.

My pay? A rich 50 cents per hour.

I would work five days a week, plus Saturday mornings, and I remember well my first paycheck was for $19.64, with all the taxes removed for the government. It should be noted that this is a time when the telephone bill was about $2.60 per month.

It didn't matter. I was working. And it would just be temporary—until something else—something better—came along. I just knew the *New York Times* or *The Washington Post* was just waiting to hear that I was available.

It was generally a one-woman office, with the exception of the linotype operator who came in to set type for us in the afternoons. He had been associated with the newspaper for many years, but his real job was as a rural mail carrier, so he came into the office after 2 p.m. each day. If the machine gave him trouble, as it sometimes did, he might be there until the wee hours of the morning finishing his work.

I had an insatiable appetite to learn all I could.

My favorite thing in that office was an old-fashioned rolltop desk, with 14 pigeon holes for all my notes and things. My only writing job was in the preparation of classified ads and the writing of social news. For those who may not be aware, that's all the news about who came to whose house for dinner, or who was having visitors, or who hosted the ladies' church group this week. Also included in that category were weddings and births.

While I was fully aware of the importance of this writing, I really was not fulfilled by all of this. I decided I had to reach out, expand my horizons. I knew it would not be easy to prove myself. No one knew my potential, least of all me.

One of my first suggestions to my new boss was the idea of introducing a school page in our newspaper. He thought it was a good idea, and together we met with school officials to get it started. Mascot for the school was the Trojan, so we called the school page, The Trojan Torch. Not entirely original, but it really garnered the readership. Everyone seemed to like it.

By June, I wanted to grow even more.

In a matter of the first six months of my employment, I had the linotype operator show me the fundamentals of running that machine. He was hesitant at first, but he found I was truly sincere about learning and the lessons were then given on a regular basis.

One of the most serious problems occurring with the linotype, which includes the use of hot lead, was not having the "line" of type fully completed. If you sent that line into the machine without the proper amount of spacing bands, it would create what we called a "squirt." Once that happened and hot lead poured out all over the place, it was a major repair job.

My first experience with that occurred when no one was around to help me. By the time I had the mess cleaned up; you can rest assured that from that point on, I would check and double check to see that the line was completed with the right amount of space bands. It only happened twice in all the time I was learning. And no one suggested that I stop trying.

This job, too, was not quite satisfying.

So, I asked to be taught how to run the small job press. It is on this machine that we print stationery, imprint envelopes, print flyers, and other such devices.

That experience also brought a hard lesson. This was more costly to repair however, than with the linotype. I learned to put in the fresh ink and clean off the press when the printing was concluded. The color of ink most often used was black and because it is a more moist ink, you could leave it in the ink well longer. Colored ink dries more quickly and must usually be removed from the well as soon as the job is done.

My memory of this experience is as vivid some 40 years later as it was the day it occurred. I was to print posters which required red ink. It went quickly—there weren't a large number of them. When it was lunchtime, I determined I would take a break and clean the press when I returned.

In less than an hour, the color had hardened and dried to the point it could not be removed from the ink rollers. When my boss saw it, he was more tactful than I think I would have been in the same situation. He let me know how much the replacement rollers would cost. He said he hoped I would not let it happen again. It was a costly lesson. But it was well learned.

I was furious with myself.

My only other negative experience with a job press was not quite as costly—but it was certainly painful.

Later, the job press of this type—a Kluge—was manufactured with an automatic feed. At the time I was a student of the printing industry, the items were fed by hand. Over a period of time, one developed a timing system, so that with one hand you removed the printed document and with the other, placed a clean sheet in its place. It was a rhythm. At one time in my life I was not very well coordinated, but I was pleased with the way I had caught on to this system. I even found myself doing the work, setting it to music in my head. It was easier to keep the rhythm going in these instances.

Well, on this occasion, I was printing envelopes. Somehow my timing was just a few seconds off, and my hand stayed in the press too long. It was caught, and the press stopped automatically. I was thankfully smart enough not to jerk my hand away, which is a natural instinct. I just wasn't quick enough to do it. My hand was released and there was a dent in it for a long period of time. No broken bones, just bruises which healed sooner than my pride.

Even though I was growing in the job, I wasn't writing.

I wanted to write.

Not just social items and meeting notices. But real reporting.

My boss and publisher, Bill Ferguson, wanted to help. He was a teacher before becoming a publisher and he did what he could, but he realized he did not have the time to do it justice. I think he sensed in me a desire to soak up all the knowledge I could. And, even then, I would want to know more. He encouraged me to learn as much as I could.

He was well aware that he could not give me a notebook and pencil and send me out into the real world. There was no way I was ready for that. While I wanted to make a difference in my community, I was frightened of the prospect of stepping into a world for which I was unprepared.

It was a dilemma for certain.

And then in the spring of 1962, the door of opportunity opened. I had been "on the job" for about a year. Was God at work here?

Iowa State University at Ames had a new leader in the journalism department. His name was Carl Hamilton and he wanted to provide a program for community newspaper people who might not have the chance or the financial means to attend college, but who needed some basic skills in news writing, law and ethics, and advertising sales, to be of value to their employers.

It was a pilot program. Untried. Unconventional. But Hamilton corresponded with newspaper publishers in the state, asking if they had people on their staff who would be interested in participating. My publisher asked me about it. It would mean nine weeks away from the office, actually living on campus and taking part in a series of intensive courses. No pay.

I did not want my excitement to show. My publisher agreed to pay for the course, if I would agree to stay with him for two years after I completed the course.

That did it. Even though it meant no paycheck, I had some funds in savings to tide me over. My mother had earlier that year suffered her first heart attack, so it was up to my sister and me to provide the funds. With what I had in savings and what my sister was making, we thought we could do it. It would be tough. I could not come home during that nine week period, because we could not afford the bus fare. Phone calls would be permitted only once a week, but I had to pay for them.

We agonized over it. We figured and re-figured. I could do it if I could get along on $20 per week spending money. My mother was excellent in working with a budget, and she said she would handle the finances. While I had never been away from home or away from my family more than a week at a time, we knew there might be homesickness with which to deal.

In the end, the fact that sold us all was that it was an opportunity for me to acquire the basic education I would need to follow my dream. Everyone agreed that we believed I had natural God-given writing ability, but it needed to be cultivated.

This was a way to do it.

When the time came, I was ready.

Goodbye, folks, I'm off to college.

CHAPTER TWO

A year before leaving for college, I had convinced my publisher I would like to write a column.

"There's nothing in our paper specifically for young adults," I told him. He encouraged me to write samples of the type of column I wanted to do, and he would decide.

I was nervous about it. I wanted it to be "just right." Once I was in print, with my own byline, I knew I could prove myself as a serious writer.

When the samples were prepared, he took them home "to study them," he said. There is no way I slept that night. I was certain my entire career rested on whether or not he believed I had some talent, real or imaginary. At that moment of my life— at the ripe age of 17 years—my world of experience was narrow. My value judgments of good and bad journalism were based on television and the movies. I felt I had a basic knowledge of what was right and what was unacceptable in polite society but, inside my heart, there was also a burning desire to write about truth, love, and of course, the American dream. My dream. It took a few years for me to realize that not everyone had that same desire for justice and equality.

Life is truly a hard taskmaster. And a very demanding one.

But, in mid-1961, I was terribly naïve and very much a believer that if one is honest and sincere, good things will come. I awaited the verdict on my column.

The publisher usually came to the local office each day, late in the morning. That particular morning had to be the longest in my life. Patience has never been a virtue for me. I paced the wooden floor and wondered if today might just be the day he would come earlier than usual.

And, strange as it may seem, I never once believed he would reject my ideas.

The worst I thought he would do is suggest we wait until I had some real experience under my belt (so to speak) and then try again, or I thought he would offer suggestions and ask me to try again, because he was a kind and gentle—yet firm—man.

I was ready to accept that.

However, neither of those things happened.

As I recall, he was later than usual coming to the office that day and I was nearly beside myself with anxiety and impatience.

He entered the office, placed his file on the desk and began checking through his messages. He asked questions about each one and then started making telephone calls. He stayed his time, doing his work, giving me instructions for the rest of the day and then appeared to be on his way out the door to return to the home office.

I wanted to shout, "Wait!", but as I stood to call to him, he turned back into the office, his hand still on the doorknob.

"Oh, yes," he smiled. "Your column ideas. I read them over last night. You show great promise. Let's talk about designing a standing head for it and introducing it at the end of the month. How's that sound?"

How's that sound? HOW'S THAT SOUND?!

I was excited beyond words—one of the few times in my life I found myself absolutely and totally speechless. I knew he could tell by the sheer joy on my face that I was truly delighted.

"One more thing," he said before he left. "Think about how often you want to write this. Writing a column every week can be strenuous and demanding with the other duties you have. Are you up to the task?"

With that, he left.

Up to the task? UP TO THE TASK?! Was he kidding? Why...why...I had more ideas in me that were ready to explode! There were things I wanted to write about. Things I wanted to question. Things I wanted to critique. Things I wanted to challenge. Not only was I up to the task, but at that precise moment, I believed that my little column could easily become the next most-quoted syndicated (even though I wasn't entirely sure what 'syndicated' meant) commentary in the country.

But working to make the dream a reality was not as easy as even I had thought. After some consideration, we decided to call the column, "Teen Corner," written by a teenager for teenagers. Subject matter was to be things appealing to teenagers of the time—food, movies, music and famous personalities. In fact, the first in my series of masterpieces dealt with—of all things—pizza.

Remember it's the early 1960s. Pizza was coming into its own as the food society's youth loved most. It seemed fitting that a new column would be launched by discussing a new, up-and-coming fad. At this time there was not the public concern or awareness about the social issues such as drug and alcohol abuse as was to manifest itself in later times.

At this early stage in my writing career, pizza seemed a safe enough subject.

It should perhaps be stressed at this point in time that, since I was working in the town where I had been raised, it was difficult for many of our readers to recognize that I might have some talent. I had gone to school with some of our readers' children. I had attended church with them. My school career had really been non-descript, so the fact was that I was constantly attempting to prove myself to the people in my community. In later years, I began to think I would never be successful in their eyes. Thirty-plus years later, I think I am, in my own way, still trying to reach that goal – to attain their approval.

As I made plans to go to college that next summer, I asked my publisher if I might continue to write the column while I was at school. I could give reports about what we were doing, about what it was like on campus and what I might hope to accomplish once I returned to work. He agreed. So without missing a beat the column continued on a weekly basis while I spent nine weeks in Ames, learning about community journalism. The column title was temporarily changed to "Life at Iowa State."

Remember now, with the exception of attending a week at church camp, my experiences away from home and family had been non-existent. A relative took my mother and me to the campus, as we still had no car. On campus that first day, I came face to face with Carl Hamilton, who was then head of the Department of Technical Journalism, and the eight other young adults who were taking part in this pilot program. We were guinea pigs and we knew it. We knew if we failed, the program would fail. Carl Hamilton spent much of the time talking with my mother, who knew the Hamilton family from the time they were youngsters. I wasn't certain if that was something to be glad about or not. I was amazed from the outset with his total recall. He could remember names and faces from last week, last year or 30 years ago. It was a trait I would try all of my life to emulate, with only a small degree of success, and one I had to attempt to recapture when I lost it later in life.

I met my roommate for the first time, a girl from a town of which I had never even heard, but a town much the same as mine—small. Class members ranged in age from 23 to my 18 years. Two of the students were children of small town publishers who intended to follow in the family business.

There were four women and five men. We were given our class schedules—news writing, advertising layout and sales, law and ethics and photography. We were warned the studies would be intense, but there should be plenty of time for leisure activities, too.

I had made up my mind before arriving at Iowa State that I was being given a golden opportunity with this adventure and I was determined to give it my best.

Unexpected on this adventure was the exercise I would be getting. The journalism building was on the east side of the campus and the dorms and cafeteria were on the west. While the campus was not as broad as it is today, it still meant walking a mile one way to classes, a mile back to lunch, then a mile back to class, and a mile to the dorm when classes were done. The weather was beautiful most of the time so it wasn't really a chore and the fresh air, though hot, was welcome after studying or working most of the day inside.

I was excited. Scared, but excited.

Truthfully, I was fascinated with the idea of learning photography. I felt that was a personal weakness, which needed a great deal of development. The instructor was a tough taskmaster. He felt some might progress faster than others—and, of course, he was right. So, he presented us with a list of assignments we would be expected to complete by the end of the nine-week period. This included animal photos, people pictures, and concluded with a series of photographs which told a story.

We spent the first day taking photographs of just about anything and everything, so we could begin the process of developing the negatives and making usable prints for publication. As part of our schedule, we were to be applying our writing and photographic skills on the job as we were summer employees for the campus newspaper, the Iowa State Daily.

My introduction to the dark room facilities was one of complete awe. At that time, though I felt I was trainable, the whole idea seemed almost beyond my comprehension. Timing and temperature was all important. It was vital that the chemicals be the right temperature, and that the time the film spent in the chemicals be not a second too long or too short. As I progressed and comprehended more and more of the procedures, I found it was something I enjoyed. I have to admit, however, that it was something for which I would never win any prizes. My photographic skills were adequate, if not mediocre by professional standards. In fact, in later years, I would come to call myself "a writer who takes pictures." I never have referred to myself as a "professional" photographer, though it was part of the work I did.

It didn't take us long to recognize that our photo instructor liked pictures of geese. In fact, he had a collection of them. As ISU tradition had it, a few geese enjoyed the habitat at Lake LaVerne, which is part of the Iowa State campus. I spent much of one afternoon taking photos of the geese on the lake, thinking these would suffice for the animal pictures required for the course—and might be appealing to the instructor as well.

I took these pictures, developed the film, and was ready to make prints, only to discover they are not considered "animals" but "fowl" and did not qualify for the assignment.

To say that I was disappointed is an understatement. Those photographs are some of the better ones I have taken, and I still have the negatives somewhere in the file.

In a desperation move, I awoke early one morning and walked to the cattle barns and took photos of the steers housed there for the agricultural program. They were good photos and qualified for the assignment, but I will never be convinced they are the better of the two groups. With the white markings on the cattle, they made for some interesting shots. I was pleased but I learned a valuable lesson that the easy way is not always the right way.

Because of the work we were assigned regarding photography, we took more than one field trip to learn about lighting, framing and content of our photographs. One memorable field trip was one made to Hardin County, particularly to the Alden and Iowa Falls area, where Carl Hamilton still owned an interest in the Iowa Falls newspapers.

It was a beautiful day, and I was so impressed with the sights and sounds of the area, I predicted I would return to Hardin County someday. Little did I know at the time how true that prediction would be? At the time, I knew very little about Eldora, which is the Hardin County seat, except that it was the location for the State Training School for Boys. Of all the field trips we made, that provided me with the best photographs of the summer—particularly those taken along the Iowa River.

We were given writing classes, which were then followed

by specific assignments for the classroom as well as the newspaper. One classroom assignment was the preparation of an article concerning population trends for our community and home county. It accented the importance of total and complete research. That article was then returned to our hometown newspaper for publication. I was so pleased when that appeared in print. Since that time I have completed several stories based on statistics and similar research, and every time I recall the instruction we received concerning how important it is that those details be accurate.

I was fascinated with the work associated with the Iowa State Daily. One particular story I completed was not long, but involved a telephone interview with an Iowa State student who was competing in the Miss Iowa contest. She was a runner-up, as I recall, but the musical number she sang which caught the judges' eye was "Hey, Look Me Over." The story and interview were not spectacular, but the experience taught how one phrase, the opening paragraph, can make or break a story.

As I recall, the sentences at the beginning of the story stated that the student had performed a song-and-dance routine to the music of "Hey, Look Me Over." The paragraph concluded by saying that the contestant's measurements were 36-22-36.

It did not take me long to realize that my area of expertise was in the writing of feature stories. It is an ability that has manifested itself over and over again in the last 30-plus years. In fact, I was surprised to discover that many people have difficulty with this type of writing. I find it comes fairly easily to me and that it is something I truly enjoy doing. I can handle the daily rigors of writing what is called "hard" news—the city council meetings, school board meetings, law enforcement reports, etc., but the true satisfaction is writing a feature story about someone who might not ever have the opportunity to appear in the news columns of our newspapers, except for a special hobby or event in his/her life. There's a real joy in that, and it embodies a type of journalism which goes beyond routine reporting.

Perhaps one of the more interesting courses to me was that of law and ethics, taught by Jim Schwartz, who would follow in Carl Hamilton's footsteps as head of the journalism department at Iowa State. Boring to some, it would set the tone of the future for me as I—more than once—came face-to-face with the idea of the people's right to know. In many instances later in my career, I would call on the knowledge I gained from that class to get me through the arguments about open meetings and what is classified as public information. In fact, it was shortly after returning to my hometown and full-time work on the newspaper there that I was to encounter an experience which, because of the information I had received at Iowa State, made it possible for me to provide public awareness on an issue vital to the residents of the community. But that will be covered in a later chapter.

Least interesting to me was the class on advertising sales and layout. Contrary to what one might think, I really did well in this class, but it was not the portion of newspaper work which carried my greatest interest. We had the opportunity to work on make-believe advertising accounts, as well as with actual accounts for the Iowa State publication. Again, it was an experience of physical endurance, because there were no public transit buses and we had no cars at our disposal, so we were subject to foot power as we went into downtown Ames to try to sell advertising.

During the summer, the Daily actually is printed weekly, and therefore, we spent Thursdays and Fridays dealing with our advertising sales for the next week. It was during one of these trips that we thought about renting a bicycle for the weekend and doing some exploring in the Ames area—in between doing our laundry, writing letters, and, of course, completing our homework. Once we figured up how much it was going to cost, however, we quickly gave up the idea. On my $20 per week allowance, there was no possible way I was going to afford that sort of treat.

It was our exposure to working on the Daily which first introduced me to a young graduate student, Tom Emerson, who also would later head the journalism department at Iowa State. A talented writer and editor, it is no wonder that his work at the university promoted him to this position. He knew and understood from the beginning that we were different from the regular students. We had more than a vested interest in seeing this program survive; we were betting our livelihoods on it. Most of us would not have the opportunity to attend college on a regular basis ever again. We were building a future for ourselves and for every small town newspaper in the state.

I was overtly aware of the importance of my own success. I wanted to glean every bit of information I could, whether or not it might ever be critical to my reporter's career. I knew beyond the shadow of a doubt that this was my chance, my opportunity to gain knowledge and skills that could provide a lifetime career in a field that I loved—writing. At the time, I had no idea I would not remain in the newspaper business forever. I had dreams about radio broadcasting, too. No thoughts at all about religion as a career. But there was always the chance that my brain might contain the words and formula for putting together the All American Novel. Someone is destined to do it. Why not me?

Perhaps more than the other students that summer, I kept mountains of notes and transposed them later for a permanent record. I still have those notes, and have been known to refer to them now and then. I was aware that my entire future in the newspaper field may depend on how successful I would be in this course

Because it was a new and different approach to community journalism, a feature article appeared in *Editor and Publisher* magazine, a trade journal for people in the business. That article said, "For nine weeks, the students are receiving a heavy dose of instruction and experience that the busy community newspaper editor doesn't have time to dispense to new staff members."

Carl Hamilton was quoted to say, "Job opportunities each year outnumber our journalism graduates, so that we can't produce enough graduates to staff Iowa's community newspapers and satisfy all other demands. But we feel we can upgrade the talents of young persons joining the staffs of small newspapers by giving them a running start, packing into nine weeks some of the things that might take them a few years to learn on the job."

Also, "It is possible, too, that older persons will be included in the group. One publisher thinks so highly of a man in his back shop that he'd like to bring him closer to the managerial end of the operation but simply doesn't have the time to retrain the man.

"Still another publisher says there is a good salesman in his town that'd make an excellent ad manager for his paper if the salesman could get a quick education in newspapering through this course."

No doubt, it is obvious that I have been an advocate for this short course over the years, though it no longer exists. The principle which brought it into being is still most valuable for those desiring to learn. In one of the columns I wrote while on campus, I talked about being a participant in a radio broadcast over WOI radio—the campus station—in which I was called upon to discuss the short course. The experience nearly ended my dreams about news broadcasting—especially after I heard the sound of my own voice.

One of the more interesting stories I was given to explore was that of superstition about the Zodiac sign which graces the entrance to the ISU Memorial Union. When it was constructed, the figures in the sign were upraised in the floor. The contractor believed that after years of students walking over the sign, it would be level with the marble flooring. That did not happen.

Shortly after its completion, the idea was spread across campus that if a student walked across the sign just before an exam, he or she would fail the exam. I watched as students unconsciously walked around the sign, and I interviewed them about it. Almost 80 percent of the students I interviewed said they really did not believe the superstition, but they weren't going to take any chances on the next exam.

One could hardly blame them.

Life in the dormitory at Iowa State was a new experience for me. In fact, having a roommate other than my sister was a new experience. Neither turned out to be bad experiences, however. I began to organize my schedule, doing my laundry at certain times, and ironing at certain times, and leaving a certain amount of time for leisure as well.

We ate cafeteria food most of the week, except for Friday nights, which we called our treat night. In Ames, not so very far off campus was a little place called "Henry's Hamburgers" which I believe was the forerunner to the McDonald's or Burger Kings that we know today. Each Friday evening they offered five hamburgers for $1. Obviously, these were no "Big Macs," but it was a special treat for us to walk to Henry's and share the cost of the burgers, and then each of us would have one, plus one fourth of another. Needless to say, at those prices, my weekly allowance was usually adequate. I do remember spending several quarters in the vending machines for things I'm not certain were nutritious but really added some spark to cafeteria food.

Graduation day came. It was a lovely ceremony that day, with each of us receiving a special "graduation" certificate and a gold pica pole—a ruler containing all the proper measurements for newspaper columns and ads—which had our names engraved on them.

I know exactly where this "golden pole" is today and I take it out now and then, just to look at it.

It was with mixed emotions that morning that I packed up all the things I had gathered in those nine weeks including the untold knowledge and began the trip home. I felt good about what I personally had accomplished there. It never occurred to me that what I had now acquired would not be enough to carry me through the rest of my career. In fact, I was confident that I was equipped with all the necessary tools and skills to make it work.

While I was sorry to part company with my new-found friends, we vowed we would stay in touch. As is true with many youthful relationships, we never did keep in touch.

In the meantime, I was ready.

Ready—and willing—to get back to work.

After all, I had crusades to launch and newly-set goals to accomplish.

I was educated.

CHAPTER THREE

Ambitious, aggressive, and somewhat arrogant would better have described my behavior in those early days, certainly not "educated."

If anyone would have told me then that God had a hand in this journey, I would have laughed. It was MY talent, MY skills that brought me to this point. I would prove to everyone who had ever doubted that I could make it, that I could be a success. A prominent and respected writer. This was just the first step to a number of great things to come my way.

I do know now, however, that without a doubt God was teaching me lessons I would need in the years which were to follow. There is also no doubt that we were traveling together on a road which is a part of life not recorded in books. It is also true I was unaware of this traveling companion. His presence was not made known to me for several years.

In journalism, many of a reporter's personal writing standards are provided through a stylebook or a list of ethics which helps to keep him/her out of the courtroom as a participant. We were warned early about the necessity of knowing what is acceptable and what is not acceptable in order to toe the line against a libel suit.

But, more than that, there are issues which we address on an individual basis, almost daily. Issues for which there are no handbooks or rules. These are experiences where we, as Christians, must follow our heart, not our head. And there are no textbooks to prepare us for it.

Scranton, remember, was a small town and much of the routine of life there involved weddings and funerals and births. Few crime stories, other than vandalism now and then, a few major fires, and certainly never any murders. Those things happened in the bigger cities. It was 1963 and everything was good. I was soon to learn, however, that even in small towns there are people and things that happen which could occur anywhere and to any one.

This story is one of an ambitious young reporter, anxious to prove herself to the community and convinced she had the tools to get whatever she wanted in the way of information. The people's right to know had to be protected, and that is just what I was going to do.

For years, the newspaper had relied on the city clerk to provide the news about the city council. No one reported about their meetings in person. News accounts from the city council came from interviewing the city clerk after the meeting was over, or were taken from the minutes whenever they happened to be typed and ready to be published. It seems nothing ever occurred at these meetings, so why bother? Well, that was all about to change. I was going to cover the city council meetings in person. I was going to tell all.

At the first meeting, I sat up front where I could clearly hear. About half way through the meeting, the mayor asked, "And,

Virginia, why are you here? Do you have some complaint or concern?"

I assured them I did not, but that I was there to cover the meeting for the newspaper. A hush went over the meeting hall. "Is there something wrong?" I asked.

The mayor quickly recovered, and said, "No. We just think it's strange you would want to cover our meetings. Nothing much happens here."

"Let me be the judge of that," I smiled.

Needless to say, they awaited with a great deal of anticipation the publication of the story in the next edition of the newspaper. They needn't have worried. There was no great expose about what the city council was doing.

But they remained nervous as the months went on. I was asked not to sit in the front row, as "it made people nervous" and afraid to talk. So I moved to the back of the room, but was still there. With each passing month, I thought they would get used to me, but somehow they didn't.

And then it became apparent why.

A relatively new mayor and council had taken office, and they wanted to make some changes. Changes which would have been good for the community. But their methods were a little questionable.

Now it should be understood that nothing happened here that hasn't happened in dozens of other cities and towns across the nation. The difference here was that I was a little naïve and "green around the gills," so I wanted to "do what I thought was right" for the people of the community.

It turned out to be a community-wide pavement project. Now remember, it was a small town, and while the project would benefit the entire community down the road, it was not without its costs. They were planning to pave all the streets in town, with the cost to be assessed back to the property owners. It was a huge price to pay, and they secretly made a pact to go ahead with it, despite what may come out at the public hearings.

First of all, it was a great undertaking which was not going to get done in one year. Plus, it was an enormous amount of debt. So, editorially, I spoke out against it. I said it was a good plan, but it was too much of a project to take on all at once, leaving the city with no debt ceiling. No possible way to take on a debt in case of an emergency. It should be undertaken a little at a time, I said.

That was the beginning of a terrible time in my life. I received threats, I had nightmares, and life became nearly impossible. These council members were still likely to think of me as a kid, having grown up in this community, and being a woman didn't help much. They should have been able to apply a little pressure and I would knuckle under. It didn't happen, and my publisher said he supported me, which gave me the courage to go on.

Well, the public hearings were held, and an overwhelming majority of the community fought against the project unless it was cut back. The council had to listen, and cut back on the project. Today, it is a community which has all paved streets, but there is little community left. It has gone the way of many small communities over the years. People leave and never come back.

One night I had a nightmare that exceeded all the other nightmares. It was the type of town where everyone kept their doors unlocked at night—no need to fear. And, it was not unusual for people to walk by themselves after dark. In the spring it was particularly nice to walk in the evening. At the time, we lived in a big old house across the street from the school house. A favorite tree for kids to play in was located on the playground. The tree, huge by all standards, was directly across the street from our house.

In my dream, I was walking home at night from either working too long or attending a meeting or just taking a stroll. It was dark, and though there was a street light on the corner, I did not see the man behind the tree. I remember looking him directly in the eye, seeing the face of a familiar council member, a gun, and standing in cold steel fear. He shot, I fell—and then I woke up in a cold sweat, breathing hard. It never reached that dimension, but I was young and under the influence of television programs about these things. I believed it could happen. I believed my life was at stake. I prayed profusely after each occurrence of the nightmare. It was not until several weeks later that I came to the realization such a thing was probably not going to happen and that anger doesn't always mean violence will occur.

It was 1963, after all. It was not a time, as it was to become 35 years later, when guns were used to settle all differences. When a problem at work resulted in a moment of gunfire. When a bad relationship would mean blasting people to death. Or when a disagreement with a teacher meant wiping out all the people in the school yard.

It was the year of the assassination of U.S. President John Fitzgerald Kennedy, and that was such a tragedy in our American society, that people today can remember what they were doing on that day, November 22, 1963, at exactly the time the word came through that President Kennedy had been shot. Not your typical day. At least not in 1963.

But, in my mind, it was a real happening. I did not quit. It was too important. Not the street pavement, but the principles involved. Good journalism, good reporting. I was right about that. And I knew it. I had experienced my first episode of protecting the people's right to know. To let the people know when their elected officials were attempting to undertake an expensive project without the public's knowledge.

Oh, there were threats to my life, to be sure, but it was an attempt to scare me aware. These people were adults when I was in junior high and high school, and that is how they thought of me. In this instance, however, I grew up right before their eyes. I gained a new respect, though it also earned me a few enemies in the process. It was a respect that came through a very real education process and which required a very high price. I learned much.

In the process I learned for the first time in my life, where to turn in times of trouble. It was subtle enough, but it was very important. Turning to God in a moment of prayer was vital to getting through the process. Unfortunately, what this part of my journey taught me was that because I was right, I was sure God was on my side and would take care of me. I was confident that such was the case. It never occurred to me that the opposition was praying to God, too. Life was just too black and white for me to think about that. In "doing what was right" I had a misguided sense of self-righteousness. Forgetting that there is a human element involved. I was so arrogant that I had convinced myself nothing could go wrong as long as God was with me.

It was a journey that I was to travel many miles before coming to a different realization.

I was traveling on a road that seemed like smooth sailing. I had other crusades, of course. I fought liquor by the drink in Iowa, to no avail, and that would come back to haunt me one day. I had my opinions on a variety of subjects, and by the time I left my hometown paper in 1966, I had established a bit of my own personality within its pages. As my farewell column said,

"I'm going. But without tar and feathers and under my own power." It was as though I had to get one last barb in to those who fought me when I knew I was right.

There was a caution light on my journey at that moment, but I didn't see it. Maybe I didn't want to see it.

CHAPTER FOUR

It was a new town, a newspaper with a larger circulation, and the interview for this new job was a little bit short of bizarre.

A March blizzard had prevented the first interview from taking place, but a week later I made the trip accompanied by my mother to a community called "Eldora". If ever I was sold on a place, it was this one. The drive into the community was beautiful, with a gateway of trees providing a beautiful canopy, even though there were no leaves. It was a beautiful welcome into the area and was probably the first selling point on the community.

It seems the major decisions of my life have been made instantaneously. I knew. I knew they were the right choice for me at the time. You have to understand what that means. Although it may seem I have a courageous heart, I don't. I stumble from one thing to the next, wondering if it was the right thing to do, worried about the consequences. That's the way it's been all my life—with the exception of three times when I took the bull by the horns and instantly said, "Yes." With no looking back about what might have been.

This was one of those times.

I approached this interview with a certain amount of nervousness. I had only talked to the publisher of this newspaper on the telephone. I could only imagine his appearance. As I went into the office, I could see that about half of the staff was there as it was Saturday. The newspaper is one which is published twice a week, so only a portion of the staff is on duty on weekends.

It turned out the publisher was actually two people – partners, in fact. There's no doubt in my mind they knew I was nervous. My initial impression of those guys was a wonderful one. The partnership consisted of an older man, a veteran of World War II sporting a large cigar and his young protégé who was in the process of becoming the sole owner, purchasing his partner's share of stock.

However, none of that was obvious at the time. The older fellow whom I will call David (not his real name) pretty much was under control during this interview. The younger fellow made the initial presentation, but David talked with me about what would be expected of me and gave me the "grand tour" of what was to be my new community.

Now this town was obviously a "big" city to me. Coming from a community of 800 people to a city of well over 3,000 was a big change, but it was a stopping place on my way up the ladder of success. I thought my journey would eventually take me to a small daily, or even to radio broadcasting. It seems strange to talk about that now, but I knew television would never be for me; I knew how that worked. My face was definitely more ready for radio than television.

We took a tour around the community; it was wonderful to have a grocery store, clothing and shoe stores, and a Ben

Franklin store all in the same town. While our small community had a variety store, the inventory was limited. Most appealing of all was the addition of being in the area where a state park was located. Beautiful. It consisted of two lakes, known as Upper and Lower Pine Lake, lots of golf, fishing, hiking and picnics.

It turned out that this pair of publishers created a new position for me; they called it county news editor. They said they really wanted me on their team. I guess they did. They were willing to pay me $100 a week. Remember, it's 1966 and I'm a woman.

As we traveled back home after a wonderful experience, Mother and I talked bout whether or not to accept. I told them as I left that I would let them know on Monday what I had decided. My sister still had to be consulted.

In fact, it should be noted here that my mother had experienced two heart attacks prior to this time and lost her employment at the bank. Remember, it was before employees had rights. She accepted it fairly well and started her own bookkeeping service, but it never seemed to get off the ground. People who might use her services already were associated with an established firm, and, at that time, not many utilized a bookkeeping service.

So, she was ready to move to a community where there were more job opportunities. My sister was working part-time at the public library at home. For two young, single women, we also knew there was not much for our future if we remained there. It's unfortunate one has to express these truths about the country's small towns, but it is truth. No matter how much we may love these small communities because of their safety, and their caring for one another, there tends not to be much of a future for the youth. I loved this town. After all, I had been born and raised here, but I knew if there was to be a journalism career for me, I would have to leave.

As I reminisced about my five and one-half years there, I recalled the young man with whom I had been in love. It turned out to be a wrong choice, as, during the Vietnam crisis, we argued about our country's involvement. He was of the age for the draft, and he feared being called into military service. He did not want to answer that call and threatened to run away to Australia. He said he felt that country was more of a democracy than the United States. It seemed inevitable that we would part. We actually met when he responded to a column I had written about Vietnam. This was an important part of my life, though short-lived. I have no idea if God had a hand in this relationship or not, but it seemed for a while it was all-consuming to me. It was important for me to discover that I could love and be loved. Bill did that for me.

I still have his love letters. For some reason, I can't throw them away or burn them. Every so often, I pull them out. They are satisfying and I feel warm when I've finished reading them.

And this life experience also persuaded me to make a change. In the early 1960s, it was considered appropriate for women to stop working outside the home when they married. I knew that before I would settle down I needed to prove I could be successful at this journalism thing. That is, if I ever settled down. God never gives us a road map. We just have to trust God's guidance along the way.

So, after speaking with my sister, we made the decision to go to a new community. Basically, what I told her was, "You can stay here, if you want, but I'm going! I think you will find more job opportunities there than you will find here."

Pick up everything, lock, stock and barrel. I called the publisher, and he said to leave it to him, he would find us a place to live. Two weeks later, my sister and I left our mother at home to handle a household sale, and we took off with a U-haul trailer behind the car. I'd never pulled a trailer before. It was a wonderful experience – and scary! It rained, and rained on the trip to Eldora, and it was Sunday, the day after my sister's birthday.

We moved into a completely furnished mobile home. The mobile home park was beautiful. Each home was placed on a lot, and had a yard and a community center where residents could pick up their mail and use the clothes washer and dryer. The home we moved into was relatively new, so it was like having a brand new house.

My first day at work was the next day. I was to go into work in the afternoon. Monday was a publication day, so the staff would be busy until later in the day. I was introduced to the editor, a guy who had graduated from college, gone to military service, returning to work in journalism. Before I arrived on the scene, this fellow had resigned to accept a job in another community and then returned. The editorial policy of the other publisher went against everything in which he believed.

I was introduced to the bookkeeper, a delightful "little old lady" who also wrote a popular column about a little bit of everything, the society editor, who was also secretary to the publisher (the guy was in everything that had to do with community service), the circulation manager, and the production crew, who provided some of my most wonderful memories. The foreman was long-haired, wore unkempt clothing, and was single, an intellectual, and a strong Democrat, which inspired this Republican to some marvelous discussions and debates. The rest of the crew amounted to a father-son team, a linotype operator who was deaf, another who was very tall, and a guy in the job-printing department who was very particular about the work he produced. As I look back on it, it was a strange combination of characters. Each had his/her own specialties which made them unique – and wonderful.

For instance, the bookkeeper's column once talked about the "Three Sons Club", which she created after she had three sons. Only people who had three sons could belong; no girls were permitted. Often the column included fascinating anecdotes about one of those sons. Needless to say, it was very well received in the community. She was a true picture of a lady, with her gray hair pulled back and never going to church without white gloves and a hat. She retired from doing the book work but continued to write that column on an irregular basis. She was the best co-worker, giving me advice and breaking all the rules. She felt she was too old to be fired.

She enjoyed our coffee break time and found it difficult to get back to work. She often took her coffee cup to her desk, which was forbidden, recalling a time when the publisher walked through the office and said, "What is this? A restaurant?" She kept doing it anyway. Her stories each morning made it a great way to start the day.

Around Christmas time, the circulation manager and I would sing our own rendition of "Rudolph, the Red-Nosed Reindeer," much to everyone's chagrin. After the first few years, the rest of the employees asked us (not so politely) not to sing it again!

I had discovered a terrific new expanded family in my co-workers. At that time we had no advertising manager, the publisher (the young one) was handling advertising. Although he started at the paper as a sports writer and general reporter, he actually did a limited amount of writing. The purpose for me to be there was to relieve a portion of the responsibility from the editor (who was also sports writer).

Therefore, a new position was created. I always felt rather important because I was trusted to develop a job description for this job. And it seemed as though it were a dream come true because the main focus of the work was to develop feature stories from the communities around the county.

The editor-sports writer was a different type of man. Remember, I had worked in the smaller town as a one-woman task force. Now, suddenly, I was employed in a news room which had five other people. It took some time to get my creative juices flowing, as well as being able to control my concentration. It was easy to get caught up in all those inner office stories.

One thing about the editor which was unique was he was quite a practical joker, and he could pull these off without ever cracking a smile. He never liked me very much, and I felt much the same way about him. He felt threatened by my presence; although I thought he had nothing about which to worry.

He rather enjoyed cajoling me, however. One time, he went through the newspaper after it was printed and pointed out what he felt were my mistakes. It was done in front of everyone at the office. He said, "A is for accuracy, and don't you forget it." His eyes were angry, as if I had been responsible for publishing something that was untrue. I will never forget that humiliation. It was a good lesson for me.

He liked cigars and usually chewed on them for a while before lighting them. He was five years older than I, loved sports and pulling practical jokes. In this community there was a group of guys who loved to play practical jokes on one another, affectionately called "The Rat Pack." They would be a book all their own.

Anyway, this guy decided to pull a joke on me first thing. In the county, there lived a man who had an interest in trees. Big trees. He would find a big tree, try to get his arms around it, and have someone take his photo with the tree. Periodically he contacted the local newspaper to run his story. He was obsessed with trees. Well, all the information about this guy was left on my desk. The only thing missing from the stack was the fact that he was an eccentric. I was expected to call this fellow and do a story.

There was something suspicious about the whole thing, but I made the call, planned the interview, and then realized what was going on. I became known from that point on as "the Tree Editor.," and then they knew that I could take a joke. Not very happily, but I accepted the fact that I had been "gotten" and vowed to pay him back.

As things happened, it was my payback that backfired. He told me one day he had spoken with Gordon Gammack, a Des Moines Register reporter and columnist, and Gordon would be there at 4 p.m. that day to interview me. I laughed. "No way," I said. "Why would he want to talk to me?"

The guy, with the straightest face anywhere, assured me it was true. But, having been subjected to enough of his practical jokes, I didn't believe. I made certain I was out of the office at 4 p.m.

When I returned, imagine my surprise when Gordon Gammack was waiting for me! Not altogether a cool, calm and collected person.

In July of 1969, the editor became ill while picking up information at the county courthouse. He had a growth in his brain that was inoperable, and which had no doubt been there since his birth. He was sent home from the hospital to die. It could happen any day, or it might not happen for several years. One never knew. It was to be an agonizing time for him, in which there were no more practical jokes. He still chewed on his cigar, but never smoked them, and he took up chewing tobacco.

But God didn't take long to take him home. It was in September, while covering a high school football game, which was the love of his life. He collapsed on the field and died the next day. Sunday the publisher and I spent cleaning out his desk. We felt it might be too painful for his wife, so we packed it in boxes for a family member to collect.

As I look back, I'm not certain it was the right thing to do, but he was only 30 years old, and I was very conscious of my own mortality at that time. He left a wife and two small sons. Aside from his practical jokes and his apparent dislike for me, he taught me much about investigative reporting which would come in handy nearly three decades later. He little knew how he influenced the lives of his co-workers. He was well-liked in the community, so everyone knew that the person who was to succeed him would have to be "special."

At 25, I secretly hoped the job would be offered to me, but I knew the likelihood of anything like that happening was next to impossible. I filled in for him as the two publishers talked over what to do. Nobody had really thought he would die so soon. The entire community was shocked.

It was 1969, and at that time there were very few women in position of power in journalism. Even though there were smaller papers which boasted the publisher's wife as a "partner," few of them were involved in the actual work of the business. For me to think I would even be considered for this job was not out of reason.

As the two publishers called me into their office to discuss it, I found out later that the older one would have given me the job right away, but the younger one hesitated. David (the elder) reportedly said, "We have to give her a chance. We have to ask her, even if she says no."

So, we discussed it. I wanted it. I wanted it so badly, I would agree to almost any terms. Well, I was given the title, but no increase in pay. I was told that the community was not accustomed to having a female news editor, so I would have to prove myself. Right.

I knew I would have to prove myself to the publisher as well.

I'm convinced that no one ever tried harder than me. Again, this was a time when women were just "tolerated" in management positions. Those who were lucky enough to earn such a position were thought to be strange or weird. But that just wasn't so. I knew my heart was in this, and proving myself was beginning to be a natural routine for me.

Not only was I 'educated,' but I now had a "real" title. I had, in the meantime, convinced myself that God was not a part of this journey. God was placed conveniently on the shelf and taken down only on Sundays for a couple of hours.

I didn't need God.

What's more, I didn't want to be reminded about God. After all, hadn't I made it all this way by myself? Hadn't I worked hard to get here? There's no such thing as a spiritual being. Not in 1969. Oh, yes, it was accepted to believe in God, and I played that role, sure enough. To me, God was just a religious symbol.

I didn't need God.

CHAPTER FIVE

Little did I know then that what I would experience in the years ahead would change my life. And change it in such a way that I never thought possible.

I was pleased with the promotion and it seems it quickly went to my head. I was glad to finally have the opportunity to make editorial decisions on my own. At first, I consulted the publisher about the major choices, but it wasn't long before I just went with my instinct. Once in a while, of course, it got me into trouble.

For instance, I received a request from a reader, who indicated she could not find a pair of affordable jeans in the community. I checked into the information she included, and, of course, found it was true. Because my facts were correct, I wrote the column about the lack of affordable jeans in town. Unfortunately, I named names. And that was a big mistake.

The new advertising manager was outraged. He and the publisher held a meeting with those advertisers and agreed that I needed to send a letter of apology to each of the retail businesses mentioned, and print a retraction. I protested the retraction, because all the facts were true. But to no avail. Some of the people I mentioned were our largest advertisers, so I succumbed to the concern about our economic losses. It was a dark day. If I could do it over, I might take a different approach. Never mention an advertiser by name when it comes to a negative issue.

Another incident had me in the middle of a neighbor dispute. By taking one side over the other, I was asking for trouble. I regretted it almost immediately after it was printed. I should have my trusted my instincts that it was the wrong thing to do. Threatened with a law suit, I printed a story which contained more facts than opinion. Until the day I left the newspaper, I was periodically reminded of that indiscretion. It was a humbling experience.

Putting all that aside, I soon found I was really good at being a newspaper editor. I enjoyed the responsibility. It is a small newspaper, so editor meant being a reporter and photographer as well. I always referred to myself not as a photographer, but as a writer who takes pictures. Photography was never one of my fortes.

While at the previous newspaper, I used a twin-lens camera, so imagine my surprise when I arrived at the new city where a 4x5 Speed Graphic was being used. You know the old models. Huge, bulky cameras, including a battery pack, which is extremely heavy. These cameras used slides (4x5), so you could take two pictures, and then you had to use a new slide. It was awkward, the negatives were large, and it was just cumbersome. The photography course I took at Iowa State did not prepare me for this. There was even a Polaroid attachment for it, which we used during the county fair—no dark room needed!

It was also part of the editor's job to oversee the production of the newspaper. God did not make me a good proofreader, but that was part of my job early on. It soon became obvious that this was not going to be something I ever did well, so the assignment was given to another. A blessing!

At 27, after a series of events that brought my career up the ladder of success, things tapered off into a basic routine.

I wrote my weekly column, covered the courthouse and police beat, and worked on a variety of feature articles (which I truly loved doing) and life went on. My mother worked at the local hospital, and my sister was working at the local public library as children's librarian. All seemed well.

Or so it seemed.

I was not happy at home. I felt I was doing more than my share of being responsible. This, in fact, was not true, but somehow that is how I felt. It was just an excuse, but I didn't see it then. I was nervous at work. Nervous because I knew I had to prove myself over and over again. I lived in fear that the publisher at any given time would give me an assignment I couldn't fulfill and fire me on the spot. Today such a thing could not happen quite so easily. Most people are protected in the workplace by some good as well as some not-so-good rules. I had made a few friends who encouraged me to break away from the family, find a place of my own, and be more independent.

Put all those things together and then add one more.

I remember taking my first drink of alcohol at age 17. I didn't think about it very much, but I didn't talk with my mother about it, knowing my father's drinking had been a problem. In fact, my father was extremely violent while he was drinking, both attempting to kill my sister and beating my mother while he was in a drunken stupor.

I remember vividly when he broke my mother's back on a cast iron bed during one of those times. She was bothered with back troubles her entire life and wore a steel brace for a period of time, which my sister and I had to help her into each morning. It was dreadful.

Knowing that, one would think that the idea of liquor and its consequences would have been absolutely frightening to me, as my father's daughter.

But, it's a line you hear all the time. I can control it, I said to myself. I don't have to do what he did. It'll be different with me.

My drinking became heavier, and more and more necessary. My day isn't going well, so I need to have a drink. My boss is difficult to work with today, so I need to have a drink. A reader didn't like something I did today, so I need to have a drink. Things went well today, so I need to celebrate by having a drink. I used all the excuses there are – and then I created more.

By far my least favorite personal characteristic is my viscous temper. I would become enraged at the drop of a hat, and sometimes, for no apparent reason. Particularly at my family because I felt they were holding me back in some way. That wasn't true, but in my state of mind, I had convinced myself that was the case. I seemed "stuck."

Usually, I could be found at 4 p.m. each day at the local pub, conversing with people who seemed to be in the same situation. I told myself that I couldn't have any trouble with drinking because I never started drinking until 4 o'clock.

But the truth is nobody knew when I quit from the night before.

I came to work with the after effects of drinking all night, and now I wonder just how I was able to cope. How I was able to function. How I was able to get the work done—all as usual. I was convinced that nobody knew, that I had everyone fooled.

As I was to learn later, nothing could be farther from the truth.

Several months passed. I had gotten to the point I would leave town after work on the nights I didn't have a meeting to cover. I would go to the city and check out a new bar or lounge, often by myself. In the early 60s, such a thing would not have occurred. A woman would rarely, if ever, be seen going to a bar alone, especially with the crimes against people which we hear about in today's society.

I was confident because of the prestige I believed I held in this community and the knowledge I had about life itself. Drinking was an escape for me—totally. While in some regards I was shy about talking the small talk with someone when I was drinking I could be very oratorical. I believed the liquid in that glass gave me inner self-worth. It was a very strong belief, and one that literally took over my life. It seems I was more humorous while I was drinking, more confident, more profound in my statements.

Truth was, it was having just the opposite effect. Everyone was laughing at me, except for those who were crying for me, wondering if I would ever wise up and realize what I was doing to myself.

From 1969 through 1974, my drinking problem gradually became worse. I moved from home into an apartment. My sister was married in 1974, my mother was now working at the newspaper as circulation manager, and it seemed to me things were getting out of hand. I knew. I knew that if something didn't change soon, I was in deep trouble—with my family, friends, and at work.

One of my friends—who truly was a friend—told me if I didn't get help for this problem, she refused to hang around anymore. I denied a problem existed because I felt that she was wrong. We each went our separate ways, and she did not speak to me for over a year. They call it "tough love" now, and it hurt as much then.

At some point, I knew I had to come to the conclusion that I had hit bottom. That's essential; if I was ever want to climb out of the bottle.

Nobody pointed at me and said, "Snap out of it, kid." Nobody said, "This is the time." Lots of people gave me warnings. Lots of people tried to intervene. To no avail. What had to happen was that I had to loose something of value. That's when the reality hit home

For me, the sign I received from God (though I didn't know it then) was when I had an accident driving from one of the all-night drinking sessions. It was about 3 o'clock as I took the exit off the interstate on a particularly cold January night. I hit a patch of ice and sailed into a very deep ditch. I was terrified beyond explanation.

What would become of me?

I stumbled to a nearby farm house, where they called the sheriff's office to report the accident. The deputy who investigated the accident said, "Woman, how did you walk away from this?"

With virtually no injuries to speak of, I had walked away, though my vehicle wasn't so lucky. I've always said the Lord takes care of drunks and fools. So God does. I was an example of this statement that night.

No charges were filed. No breath test was administered. I had to call a tow truck to get my vehicle back to town, and when I finally sat in my own apartment that morning—facing the idea of getting ready for work with no sleep, plus dealing with a hangover—I was literally shaking. Never in my life have I been so absolutely scared. As I recall I reported to work on time and had managed to manufacture an excuse for the accident.

After the accident, I wandered around for day. When I finally went to the local bar and ordered a drink, I couldn't swallow it. At home later that night, I cried so much that the neighbors were concerned. What would become of me? What indeed.

Until this point in my life, I was born and raised in the United Methodist Church. When we moved I became associated with the United Methodist Church again, but during this time of crisis, I stopped being a part of the church. Since I was a freshman in high school, I had sung in the church choir – I love music and the expression of music – but all that stopped. I was a member of the city council – the first woman to be so elected – and it so happened that the director of the church choir accused me of not having my priorities straight. I tolerated him, but soon found it no longer enjoyable to be in the choir.

During this period of time, the minister was ineffective. Although I had been a regular fixture at church, I no longer was going on a regular basis, and no one ever came around to find out the reason. Perhaps they didn't know how to approach me about my problem. Perhaps they felt it would be better for the church if I weren't there. I will never know. And I, well, I was going it alone, remember? I didn't need God. At this point, I really wondered if there was a God.

Startled that I was afraid to take another drink, I went through the withdrawals. I shook, I cried, I even screamed. But I knew it had to come to an end. I couldn't go on like this. My family was important to me, and my career was important to me. Life had to change. Still somewhat in denial, I didn't want to visit the AA (Alcoholics Anonymous) group which met locally. I did not want to have anyone locally know. It would be embarrassing to my mother, I thought.

Much of the activities in which I participated while drinking would be an embarrassment to my mother—to anyone's mother. No matter the details, there is nothing among those memories of which I am proud. Every so often they haunt me. It's as if they are serving as a reminder of what used to be.

So, I worked through things. I occupied my time with more constructive issues—volunteering in a variety of ways in the community, putting in extra hours at work, and permitting myself to play very little. I call it, "being responsible." It was a successful plan, but little did I know it would return to haunt me later.

By talking about alcoholism in this manner, I do not mean to belittle or understate how absolutely dangerous a disease this is. I can't put into words how devastated I felt, and how many times I felt near suicide. My faith wasn't gone, but it was placed on hold for a long time. In my journal, I often wrote about suicide and how I was feeling. I'd lost friends, a lot of faith, and so I decided my work was the only answer worth pursuing.

And work is exactly what I did.

For the most part, few people in the community were aware of my excessive drinking. Somehow—and I still don't know how—I was able to fool them for a very long time.

Finally, at the end of a particularly full day at work, I sat at home, exhausted. Not wanting to do anything. I closed my eyes to take a little nap. As I slept, I thought about church and how I missed going. Maybe it had been just a habit, but it was a good habit, and I missed it. Technically, I was a member of the United Methodist Church, but I was nervous about starting back.

So, I continued to stay away.

Then, a couple I knew from the neighboring Quaker church asked me if I would sing with their choir for the Easter cantata.

They had a need for a solo alto. I did not hesitate to say "yes," but I wondered. I feared entering that church. I've always said it was amazing that thunder and lightning didn't flash at the sight of you-know-who coming to church after nearly four years away.

In fact, there is no way to describe how I felt as I walked into that church. Such warmth, such fellowship. I was welcome there and I could feel it in everything which was said and done in the next several weeks. I did not join the church or even continue going there after the cantata was completed, but I understood that I could now return to church.

Somehow in their open arms, my Quaker friends had shown me that forgiveness is possible. Forgiveness is freely given by Jesus Christ. And, what was more surprising to me, Jesus gives ME forgiveness. Just like that. My sins had been forgiven.

For many years—in fact, even to this day—I know how embarrassing my drinking was to my mother. And how disappointing. I can never have enough remorse for that. She had worked very hard to see that everything was all right for my sister and me. At that point, I had failed her.

A co-worker at the newspaper was editor of the lifestyle page and a member of the United Church of Christ (Congregational) in this town. She was also the choir director. She said to me one day, after the cantata was done, "If you want to sing, why don't you come sing with us?"

God works in some really mysterious ways. It was as though I was waiting for her to say the word. The very next Sunday morning I went to sing with the choir. Three years later, I became a member, and for the next 23 years, I was a faithful member of that congregation.

Thanks to those people who asked me back to church with no strings attached, warmly and sincerely. Sure, I know it was truly God at work in my life. But they were God's instruments of communication. They served God in such a way so that I would not be made less of a person if I turned around and went back to church. It was a very personal and special ministry for them to perform for me. I knew I had done wrong, but I also knew –after all this time – God forgives. It's a powerful message.

Later, I was to be given another opportunity to deal with my alcoholism, in such a way that I would never quite imagine.

In 1983, my mother died of a massive stroke. She went quickly, with little suffering, but I never had the courage to discuss this issue with her – or my sister—before she died. In fact, I never spoke of it to anyone until after her death. I was too ashamed.

In 1985, a substance abuse treatment center was established in our community. It was a very controversial decision to make it a part of the local hospital. Many in the community felt it would harm our image as a community.

So, to give them an idea of what goes on in a treatment center, I received permission to do a series of articles for the newspaper from within. Approval was given for me to spend "family week" with one of the patients and share his story. I remember telling the counselor before we started that I was there as an observer. She had been opposed to my being there at all, and said, "No one is just an observer here. Everyone participates." Family week is the time that family members of the patients have an opportunity to address their addict face-to-face, in an attempt to find out what may have gone wrong.

In preparation for writing the series, I assigned some of my duties elsewhere so that I could be at the treatment center all day. It was probably one of the most emotional experiences of my life. Face to face with the reality of it all, I came to address the issue of my own drinking. Like a mirror, my life was being spilled out in front of me. It was another's story, but it reflected my own experiences and what I had become. The first day, I wanted to run away. It took every ounce of courage I would muster to get me to stay.

I talked—for the first time—about my father and my own addiction. I met the demons head on. But I had no idea what would result. Each day when I returned to the office to compose my article, I would type furiously to get the story on paper. I could see more clearly now than ever before what my life had been like and how desperate I had apparently been to succeed.

At the conclusion of the week, the counselor presented me with a medallion which contains the Serenity Prayer—part of the AA program—and said, "You have finally dealt with your demons. Your mother would be proud."

Although I had virtually stopped drinking for over 10 years, it was then—March, 1985—that my recovery actually began. No one could have known what road I would tread next.

Only God would know.

CHAPTER SIX

The family that I spent the week observing were terribly cooperative. The counselors had approval from me to read the articles before they went to print, the subject was so very sensitive, and their methods were so very controversial at the time. I recall one of the changes made in those articles had to do with how I referred to the alcoholic. I think I had referred to him as an "inmate," as though he were in prison. Unfortunately, that is how society generally accepted alcoholics even at that "enlightened" time. She asked me to think of the alcoholic as a "patient", as though he were in a hospital.

"That's why they have to wear their pajamas until they reach a certain point in their recovery," the counselor told me. "They have a disease; they haven't committed a crime."

With her considerate guidance, I began to see myself in a different light. Not as a total failure, but as a simple human being with faults who makes mistakes. And, who, praise God, can be forgiven. Is forgiven. What an enlightenment that was! It was probably the first time in my life that I had admitted that drinking has been a problem. That drinking had been MY problem. And the first time that I came face-to-face with God as a forgiving parent. I had been taught this fact for many years, I even thought I believed it, but it was not until that moment of enlightenment that I knew it to be true.

It was an unbelievable moment. For the first time in a long time, I felt whole again. And I felt open to express myself again.

Then in the fall of 1985—two years after my mother's death, I was feeling depressed, overly tired and I had moments of total depression. I floundered around without much sense of purpose in my life. I performed my duties at work; in fact, we added some responsibilities. It was as though I couldn't do enough; I seemed to be thriving on all this work. Then I seemed to fall apart. Nothing I started was finished. I seemed to be swimming upstream, against the current.

I thought it best to seek a doctor's advice, so I went for a check-up with my family physician. I explained to him what I had been feeling, he conducted a battery of tests, and I ended the interview breaking into tears for no reason, sobbing uncontrollably. I told him I was doing that on a regular basis, and it really scared me.

He advised me that the problem most likely was with a chemical imbalance in my body, which was the cause of the depression. He prescribed some medication—anti-depressants—and said if that didn't take care of it, he would recommend a good psychologist for me to see. In talking with him, I realized that I had never permitted myself to grieve for my mother.

I had gone back to work the day following her funeral, because I knew that is what people would expect me to do. There was no time for grieving. It was best, I thought, to pour myself into my work, to do what I could to show that life was continuing, that I was OK. Funny how it always seemed important to me to do what "other people" expected of me. And to put on a good face. After all, hadn't I taken care of my mother? Hadn't I been the one to lead my family, when things got tough? I was a good care-giver, even though when my mother needed me most, I wasn't there for her.

And then it hit me like a ton of bricks.

The reason I had not grieved. I hadn't permitted myself to do that because I didn't think I deserved to grieve. In fact, I was sure I didn't deserve it. My mother needed me, but I was at a football game that day having fun. And I wasn't at home when I was needed. It was something that had gnawed at me for two years, tearing away at my reserve, yet was totally unnecessary. Perhaps I didn't deserve forgiveness, perhaps I didn't deserve to take the time to grieve, but through the grace of God, forgiveness was already mine. I had only to ask for it.

And, finally, I was beginning to get it.

It was probably around this time that the minister of the Congregational Church asked if I would like to fill in for him, preaching while he went on vacation. I had always loved public speaking, so I said that I would really enjoy it.

For the first Sunday of his vacation, I did something generic—something along the line of the Lectionary for the day—something, I'm sure—that was very, very clever. But on the second Sunday of his vacation, I took my courage in hand and decided to talk about my alcoholism—to meet it head on in this very special confrontation. My feet and hands both shook at the possibility.

After reading the scripture, I approached the pulpit and started the sermon in the Alcoholics Anonymous tradition. "Hello," I said, "My name is Virginia. And I'm an alcoholic." There was total and absolute silence. You could have heard the proverbial pin drop at that moment. It was as though the congregation all inhaled a breath at the same moment. For an instant, I thought I would panic. "Surely, they don't want to hear this now. Not one of them believes me…!"

I could see in their faces how absolutely shocked they were. Later several people indicated they had known I had a "drinking problem" but they did not think it had become that serious.

However, the best thing to come from that experience was the surprise realization that I could deliver a powerful message from the pulpit. Many comments came from the congregation telling me that I had missed my calling—that perhaps I should have been a minister! Well, with my swelled head, that was all I needed to feed my ego, and absorbed the compliments like a sponge. Oh, I knew it took a great deal of education to become a really good minister, but for a little while, I told myself that they were absolutely right.

There was a dark side to thoughts like those. While I felt good about doing a good job and accepting the compliments that came with it, I also took time—however right or wrong it might have been—to feel a little sorry for myself. (A little?)

I thought about the fact that my father had died so young, my mother had to go to work to make ends meet, my sister and I had to go to work to help support the family, my mother had her first heart attack and subsequently lost her job, and there was no chance for me to go to college full-time, and so it goes…or, so it seemed. It was at these times that I particularly felt the craving for a drink. It took all of my self-control to not walk to the nearest bar and order just that. It would take the rest of my life for me to learn some self-control as far as drinking was concerned. It was as though I were putting myself to these tests to see whether or not I could do it. And each time I was successful, I wanted to celebrate it as a victory—a victory for every person who fights with his own demons. It was a good thing.

My dealings with my alcoholism were to work in my favor in years to come, in ways that I could only imagine.

I thought after that day in church that people would avoid me, stay away from me, and no longer accept me as a social person. I had spent much time at the local country club, playing golf and drinking—whenever possible. I had certain friends who were friends because they were also drinkers. I knew by announcing my alcoholism so publicly, I was at risk to lose a friend or two.

Actually, both things occurred. I was shunned by people I had considered as "good friends," but I also was opened to begin new relationships, new friendships. They were numerous. It was as though there was a new awakening in my life. There was a whole world of possibilities, and now I was open to sharing some of them. Being an alcoholic had been difficult to deal with, and there were still times when the demons would come to me in the middle of the night, but now it seemed as though I might do something with it—something that might help others who were face-to-face with their own demons in the night.

I began to be asked to fill the pulpit more and more. Even at the United Methodist Church down the street—my former church home. And I was delighted with the opportunity.

I found myself fanaticizing about the future. I could see myself as a minister, a REAL preacher. Bringing people to God, spreading the Good News of the gospel. But even I knew it was just a dream. First of all, never could a woman expect to be ordained. Secondly, I needed an education to receive ordination. My hopes of making this a reality were all but dashed. Oh, well, at least once or twice a year I could preach and

I could live with that. Or so I thought.

I realize now that all my life it has been important to me to live it in such a way so as to make a difference. How, I'm not certain, but it seems as though I was always totally obsessed with the idea. I wanted to write the editorial that made a difference, write the column that touched someone's heart and made a difference, do a workshop that turned a young child's life around and made a difference, deliver a sermon that touched a soul and made a difference.

I was not unlike anyone else who struggled just to be remembered. When my Grandmother Stiles died at the age of 88, her son stated that "you go through life hoping you've touched someone's life, and yet when it's over, it's like your footprint in the puddle. When you lift your foot away, the water comes in and covers it again. It's as though you weren't ever there." I tried to tell him that such was not the case, particularly because I felt my grandmother HAD made a difference, frail though she was. I told him, "Yes, but the indentation made by the footprint is still there."

Not such a wise saying, but I wanted to make a point, so, I am guessing that much of what I was obsessed about was revealed by that conversation. I was like everyone else—I wanted to be remembered for having done SOMETHING, no matter how significant. I wanted my life to have made a difference.

Now I was working close to fourteen-hour days – never less than twelve hours each day. I tried to protect the weekend days, but there always seemed to be something news-related to do on Saturdays and Sundays, and I was in charge, so I needed to be there to provide the necessary news coverage. I wouldn't say "no" to anyone. I couldn't say "no" to anyone who asked me to come with pad, pencil and camera, so I went, even though I needed to be in church instead. Sometimes I didn't even bother with an excuse. I just didn't go because I was tired and needed a couple extra hours of sleep. But I soon began to meet myself coming and going. I would sleep at the office, going home long enough to shower and change clothes. It was no good and I knew it.

I thought that was what my boss and the public wanted—more and more news coverage—and it was getting to the point I couldn't provide it on my own. When I asked my publisher for help, he said, "If you can't handle it, you are just going to have to look at your schedule, see where you are giving too much, and cut back." No offer to hire another person. No offer to even hire a part-time person. I knew it was up to me, if the paper was going to continue to be successful. As much as I wanted that, I wanted something new to do, some new adventures. People get bogged down if things don't change even just a little. Even with large daily newspapers, things have to change periodically.

I was pretty much drifting aimlessly in this portion of my life. It was as though I had no purpose, no real goals, and no challenges. I wanted goals, I wanted challenges, but they just weren't materializing.

My co-workers, my minister and my publisher, kept telling me to take some time off, but I didn't see the purpose in that, so I just kept on working, night and day.

During this time—the late 80s,—I began to feel the degradation of the workplace. I started in my field as a journalist with basically no skills, expecting it would be a temporary job, lasting until something better came long. I was a woman, which made me a second-class citizen in many people's eyes, including my publisher. As a woman, it was understood that I could do all the work that my boss could dream up, and as a single woman, I better do it or I would be quickly out of a job.

Feeling as a second-class citizen was something that I never seemed to move past. I wanted to believe that I was indispensable because I was good, because I was talented, and because I was loyal to the company. Never mind all that business about freedom of the press and freedom of speech—I was LOYAL!

As the years went by, the caliber of my work was not celebrated, but expected. And expected on a daily basis. I was never supposed to feel depressed or to feel sorry for myself. I was expected to be at the top of my game all of the time—24/7 as they say today.

It soon become obvious to me that it wasn't working well at the newspaper office, and I thought perhaps it was time to begin looking elsewhere for another job. But I had to do it quietly. If my boss found out that I was searching, I knew I would be in big trouble with him, and might well lose the job I already had.

It was an exciting search. I knew that to improve my situation, I would need to seek a post on a small daily, and in management. I would have to have a salary in mind, so that I could negotiate on solid footing, if I got that far in the interview process.

So, I began advertising in the trade publications. I received a call from a newspaper in Sterling, Illinois, for the post of news editor. It looked intriguing, and I felt I was qualified for this. They asked me to come for an interview, which I did. While I loved the community and the job, they needed someone to come right away. I had agreed with my boss that if I ever left there I would give at least two weeks notice, and "starting on Monday" just didn't seem to fill that requirement.

I hate being pushed, with a passion. The interview was successful, but I just couldn't see myself pulling up stakes and moving in the matter of a couple of days. Being single didn't mean I didn't have roots, and as long as I had lived in Eldora all this time (which was longer now than I had lived in the town where I grew up) meant I had *roots.* So, I went back to the drawing board—and the classified ads.

The next interview was with a newspaper in Iowa—not far from Eldora—which would have meant a newly created position for me. It was a great interview, but the family who owned the paper had a long-standing relationship with my publisher and that seemed to be a hang-up with them. "How will Al ever get along without you, if you come here?" they asked. I wanted to shout at them, "Who cares?" but I was able to restrain myself. Consequently I lost the opportunity for that job because they just couldn't bring themselves to "take me away" from my boss.

There were others with much the same outcome. Either they weren't happy with me, or I couldn't do what it took to make the move—even though I knew I had to make changes in my life in order to save my life.

So, I stopped looking. It seemed that, though I tried very hard to find another newspaper position, this was not the right time. I even looked at other kinds of jobs, different, though related. Jobs such as in the public relations field, or as a chamber of commerce manager or something similar. But the main stopping point with those jobs was the lack of an education. I convinced myself that the timing was all wrong for the next newspaper job, so I would just sit back, relax, and wait for the timing to become better.

In the meantime, my opportunity for a new office opened up at the newspaper as major remodeling was undertaken, I took a stand (which I rarely did), and a section was fashioned in the design for the building which made it possible for me to have a private office. Prior to this we sat in a large open newsroom-style, and it was difficult to have a private conversation with anyone without the entire office listening.

In the days of linotypes and web presses, it didn't matter so much because the noise would make it impossible to hear anybody's conversations! Once the web presses were replaced by the "offset" presses, and later with the introduction of computers, things quieted down, and it was necessary to meet with people in a private setting. So, 20 years after I began working at the Eldora newspaper, I graduated to my very own private office.

I celebrated as much as I could—and the entire staff celebrated that summer with an open house noting the complete remodeling project.

In January of 1991 I would celebrate my 30th year as a journalist with a special open house of my own. I would later recall that event as a milestone which marked the beginning of the end of the portion of my life spent as a journalist.

A good journalist.

CHAPTER SEVEN

It was early into my years at Eldora that a special friend came into my life. Her name was Evie.

I had a great number of friends in my life—they came and went—but Evie was different. She came into my life with a great big smile on her face, laughing at everything that life had to offer. She hated to do all the things I loved to do. It was as though we "meshed" perfectly. Despite all of that, she and I did have a number of things in common, which is wonderful for friends to be able to say about each other. It took a time, but eventually we complemented each other, and that was a good thing.

I include her in this commentary because, believe it or not, she was part of my spiritual journey. Yes, there were others as well, but none so significantly impacted my life as did Evie. She was a high school graduate with no college credit to her name, and she was employed by the Chamber of Commerce as their executive secretary, a job she held for more than 25 years. Her mother died of cancer at the age of 42, leaving three children. Evie felt an obligation toward her brothers to provide a home for them, to take care of them.

When she and her husband, Dick, married in 1956, they provided a home for her middle brother, also named Dick. He was in junior high school at the time. Her father raised the younger son, a grade school student. Because her husband and brother shared the same name, family members often referred to them as "Little Dick" and "Big Dick", but soon had to end that reference when Little Dick grew to over 6-foot!

I met Evie as part of my reporter's beat. One of the offices I called on regularly was the Chamber of Commerce office. Through Evie I was able to meet the mayor and council as their offices were housed in the same building. It gave me an opportunity to become involved in the community, which is something my publisher wanted to have happen. He wanted all his employees to be very visible in the community where they worked and resided.

I had no problem with that concept because I was a community involvement kind of person. I was very social, and very active as a volunteer within the community. Though sometimes that involvement was not popular.

Evie and I became instant friends. At first, we would meet over coffee once a week while I discovered what was happening with the Chamber that we might consider to be newsworthy, and she learned about other things going on in the community through our little visits.

Soon we were meeting every morning for coffee at the local soda fountain. It was a community meeting place, and it was fun to exchange items of interest, not only with Evie, but other working girls in town.

Things between us weren't always peaches-and-cream however. We had been friends except for a short time when it became apparent to her that I was drinking a little more than one should. For a long time, she said nothing. Later, I thanked her for that, but today I wonder if that maybe prolonged my confrontation of it.

I assumed she took it as long as humanly possible, and then she took me aside one day. She wasn't mad at first, but it became perfectly obvious that something was bothering her. When I asked her about it, she said, "How long since you had your last drink?" I just laughed. "You're kidding, right?" When she assured me she was not, I said, "A few hours ago."

Then she was angry; in fact she was furious. "I thought so. I can still smell it on your breath."

"So…?" I asked.

"So, don't you think you are asking for trouble? You're drinking entirely too much, and too often."

I assured her I did not have the faintest idea what she was talking about. She said, "Don't lie to me. I know you are drinking every day, and for a longer period of time each day. You have to stop."

"Don't get excited," I said. "I've just had a bad week. I can stop anytime I want."

"Then do it……" she said.

"Okay, I will," I said.

As I thought about it, I came to the conclusion that I COULD stop it at anytime, and I would decide when that time would be. So I didn't stop. It was yet another lie to myself. Evie knew me well enough to recognize it for what it was.

Later, when she realized I was not going to stop, she approached me again and said, "You need help. Get some help." It was as though she were really disgusted with me. Then she threatened me with the loss of her friendship. "Get some help," she said, "or we can't be friends any more."

I didn't believe her. "You won't do that," I said.

To which she replied, "Watch me." And then she walked away.

For an entire year, she refused to have anything to do with me. Not that I blamed her, but such a gesture really hurt me. The good thing about her taking this action was that it made me stop to think about what my drinking was doing to other people.

It was something I had not thought about at all.

A year later, when she saw that I not only promised to quit but actually had stopped, she began to once again invite me to join her at coffee, and I gradually returned. It had been a long struggle between us, but some of our worst times, some of our worst experiences together, were ahead of us—not behind us. The thing that came out of my struggle with alcoholism was that it made the bond between us much stronger; it made it possible for both of us to recognize that each of us, as human beings, has human frailties, makes human mistakes, and is entitled to each other's forgiveness. Although it did not come easily.

For instance, in May, 1982, she noticed something was wrong with her glands; they seemed swollen. However, after a time, the swelling seemed to subside, so she didn't think any more about it. In September of that year, over Labor Day I was scheduled for surgery to remove a tumor on my left ovary, and I was totally scared about undergoing an operation. The doctor indicated that they would test the tumor immediately to see if it was malignant, so that just made me worry even more. I was scared. No doubt about it.

If it turned out to be malignant, I would have to undergo a series of chemotherapy treatments and whatever else might be needed. The surgery went without a hitch, however, and the tumor was found to be benign. We celebrated the good news. I remember them telling me that the tumor was benign, trying to make me hear them, as they rolled the gurney back to the room. "You're Ok," they said.

However, as Evie left the hospital room, she told me that she finally made an appointment with a doctor to find out if everything was alright, as the swollen glands had reappeared. It was later that month that she was to meet with the physician. She went through a battery of tests, the results of which were to be revealed a couple days later.

Two days later, we were sitting in the waiting room of the clinic, where her doctor's office was located. When she came out, she was white as a sheet. "They have to do a biopsy," she said. "They don't know if it's malignant or not." The next morning, she was at the hospital bright and early to have a biopsy.

Her doctor said for her not to worry, but that was like telling someone not to answer the telephone; it just wasn't going to happen.

She came out of surgery, and we knew the answer: the tumor was cancerous. Her greatest fear seemed to be realized. Her mother died of a melanoma, and Evie had told me some years earlier that she felt she would die young, all thanks to her mother. She believed in her heart that her mother's disease would be hers and that there would be no cure.

Her hometown doctor sent her to a physician at Mayo Clinic in Rochester, Minnesota, for setting a series of treatments. The doctor in Rochester assured her that things would be fine. He told her, "I don't see death in your face. You're going to be fine."

And so, with that kind of validation, Evie set out to beat the disease. She was not going to let herself be mastered by this disease. She was going to outsmart it.

She began a series of chemotherapy treatments which seemed to stop the runaway spread of the cancer. She would receive a treatment once every three weeks in Rochester, then return home and get violently ill. The doctors gave her some pills to prevent the vomiting, but nothing worked with her. She had a very sensitive stomach.

It was amazing how she coped. Many times she told me she was feeling good, when I really wondered if that was the truth. I know she became tired of my asking, but I needed to know.

Her hair began to fall out, quite slowly at first. Then one day we walked the block to the coffee shop, and the weather for the day was lots of strong winds. By the time we had walked that block, all of her hair was gone. I was sent to her house to bring a scarf for her to put over her head, so as to hide it from everyone. We used to laugh together about the loss of hair. She would look in the mirror every day to see if it had started growing back. When the hair came out, there were only two small strands of hair left, and those two strands of hair never came out! It was comical to think about it, and about how it made her look. When it came back in, it was like peach fuzz, and we laughed about that.

She had been diagnosed with lymphoma, and we were told that of all the types of cancer it was the best to have because there was a 90 percent cure rate. She had only to go five years cancer free and then she would probably be OK.

What we hadn't counted on was the heredity factor. Lymphoma was not the only type of cancer Evie had to deal with. She did go five years with good check ups, and once that was over, we began to breathe a little easier. However, the doctor informed her that because of her family health history, she needed to do regular checkups in order to keep ahead of it.

In 1990—eight years after the cancer was first detected—

the cancer came back, this time in a different form. The doctors in Rochester found a melanoma in a mole-like sore on the calf of her leg. They decided to operate right away, and in doing so, removed the sore as well as a wide area around it. When she awoke and was permitted to see the damage the surgeon's knife had done, she wept.

The doctor explained that the cancer cells had spread too far, they had to remove that amount of her calf to get rid of the cancer. She still wept. It took her a long time to accept what had happened. Until that particular experience, she had complete faith in the doctors of Rochester to eliminate the cancer. Now she wasn't so sure.

More treatments. This time radiation, over the lower part of her torso. After the first few treatments, she was burned by the radiation, so, she simply stopped. When she left Rochester on that Friday, she told them, "I will return when this has healed, or mostly healed, but not before."

So, she went home to heal from the radiation burns.

Even that was not the end of what proved to be her endless battle with cancer. As she continued to see doctors and specialists, I continued to believe in her strength. After all, she had told me she would beat it, and I had no reason to not believe her. She and Dick went back and forth to Rochester on what eventually became a regular routine. Going for treatments, returning home just in time for her to get really ill.

Always she kept up the look of gradually getting better. She not only had all of us convinced (or so I thought) but she had convinced herself as well. How deceiving it all was! How often I look back at things that were said, and things which were done—and all of them in love—that were definitely wrong. She tried to spare my feelings – so many times.

As we approached winter of 1993—11 years after the

original diagnosis—it appeared that she would need another operation. A heavy smoker all her life, the smoking had taken its toll on her body. It now appeared as though she had lung cancer, and a portion of her lung would need to be removed. In January of 1993, it was removed, and for a while, things seemed to become better.

We wanted to believe that now, perhaps, it would be over. There were frustrating moments as she still struggled, finding it ever more difficult to go to work, but she made it every day that she could, and loved it. Late in the spring, however, the board of directors of the Chamber decided—whether right or wrong—that Evie's position needed to be terminated.

She didn't tell anyone else at city hall that she was nearly done working. She didn't want them to know. Little by little she cleaned her desk of her personal things and took them home. I would pick her up at work and take her home. On that last day, I would have given everything I had to show the Chamber directors the courage she had when she stood, told everyone good-bye for the day, and walked out. When we were outside, she virtually sobbed from the weight of sorrow on her soul.

And I cried with her.

I hugged her, but nothing I could do or say helped.

She couldn't understand how, after 25 years of faithful service, her skills and capabilities were no longer needed or wanted. It came as a harsh blow. For a long time I blamed the 10 people who served on that board, that they should have had Evie participate in the ultimate decision about her leaving work. The way it was done was so very cruel and dehumanizing. She deserved better. It may well have been time for her to quit, but it was handled poorly.

As Christmas approached in late 1993, she began to put her husband's business accounts on the computer she bought during the summer. She had taught herself computer skills by reading the manual and hands-on use of the machine. She was scared by the idea of the computer, but she quickly became knowledgeable, and enjoyed working on it at home.

As the holidays came nearer, she wanted to have a real "family" Christmas, much like the ones of old, when her brothers and their families were around. So, she planned a "family" Christmas for her brothers and their wives. She worked in the kitchen for hours on end preparing the meal, near to collapse.

One of the brother's wives reportedly made the remark to her husband as they drove to their home in Omaha, "Don't you see? This was your last Christmas with Evie. She was doing this for you, knowing that she won't ever have the opportunity to do this again." He refused to believe it and shrugged his shoulders in denial. I didn't want to believe it either.

On January 31, 1994, I was called from my bed to come to Evie and Dick's house. The ambulance was there, and they were taking Evie to the local hospital. Something had gone wrong.

I knew I had no choice. I went.

Her blood count was low. In the emergency room, the doctor said, "We have to get her to a hospital where they have a blood bank available. She needs transfusions." So, while the ambulance made ready to take her to the hospital in Ames, which was about 50 miles west of where we lived, three of her friends, including myself, made ready to go to Ames for the night. It was about 9 p.m.

In Ames, her spirits seemed high. She was making jokes all over the place about all kinds of things. We left at about 4 a.m. to come home after they assured us she would be OK for the present. I never would have left that night if I would have known it was the last time I would see her alive. Amazingly, as they admitted her to the hospital there, they routinely asked if she had a living will, and she said, "We'll talk about that later." So many times she had instructed those of us who were her friends of the importance of having a living will, and yet, she had prepared no such thing for herself.

When morning came, I called to Ames to check on Evie, only to discover that they had sent her to Rochester when she took a turn for the worse during the night. She was placed on life support. Her husband and brother struggled with whether or not to turn off the machine, but finally on February 24, at 6:10 p.m., Evie died. She had been my best friend for 27 years. I wept uncontrollably.

I had told my minister a couple of weeks before she died that things were serious. I said, "I'm afraid Evie's dying."

His response was one of the worst possible responses anyone could make, or so I thought. "Of course she's dying, Virginia. Everyone knew it would happen, except for you."

My one last act for my friend was this. I paid tribute to her by writing a special column for her. It was the last thing she would have expected from me; she hated to have me write about her. It was the last and best thing I could do for her.

The words follow:

She was an independent woman of the 90s long before there was such a thing.

She swept into my life one spring day in the late 1960s, with a smile on her face. She could walk faster in high heels than anyone I ever knew; and she could not sit still, with her hands at her side.

If we were having coffee in her house, she was doing something with her hands—dusting, cooking, crocheting— something! She would say, "Don't mind me, I'm listening. I just have to get this done..."

She could get anyone I know to reveal their innermost secrets, but when it came to talking about her own—well, that was a different story. She was clever that way.

And she was particularly good at calling in favors. Even if you didn't owe her a favor, she would convince you that you did.

Let's see, do you owe me a favor, or do I owe you a favor?" she would say, and then add, "*Oh, I think you owe me a favor—I'm sure of it.*"

Never mind that you were just hoodwinked by the best. You did what you were asked. Many times more than once. In fact, once it was determined that you owed her a favor, it became a lifetime payback.

You did that last year? she would say, "*Good that makes you the man with the experience. We need that.*"

She could make sale racks of clothing appear anywhere. There might be only one such rack in the entire store, buried back in a dark corner, but she would find it. And many times, would find a bargain. She loved to shop, but did not always spend her funds on herself. She was also very good at spending other people's money.

She found bargains, yes, but she often shared those with other people. "*This would look good on you,*" she would say. "*And see, it's on sale for 50 percent off. It's you.*"

Of course she was usually just as honest in telling you if something didn't look OK. "*Are you sure you want that?*" she'd say. Looking through the other items in the area, she's pull something out of the middle of the air and say, "*Here, try this on. I think you'll like it.*"

Nine times out of ten that was the case, and you bought the item she had recommended.

But she was always wary of a so-called bargain. "If you don't need it, maybe it isn't a bargain," she would say.

For nearly 28 years, Evie Stone was my friend.

I remember years ago working in the evenings and on weekends to help type those dirty old green stencils for the annual report she prepared each year for the Eldora Chamber of Commerce.

I remember she and her husband, Dick, calling me on evening—or I should say morning—at 2 a.m. and inviting me over for breakfast. They had just returned home from a dance and were hungry. She thought I would be, too.

I went for breakfast.

In my pajamas.

I remember being around to oversee as she and Dick trimmed the poplar trees and hedges around their house. I didn't do anything, necessarily, but in my own way I assisted. These acts were only performed on Sundays or holidays—Dick insisted.

I remember sharing secrets; telling jokes; laughing as she literally licked her plate clean; and watching as she downed an entire pitcher of root beer and ice cream, sharing one glass with me. She said, "The doctor said I need the calories."

She made no effort to remove the ice cream-and-root-beer moustache.

Nor did I want her to.

There was no way for us to know during the early morning hours of January 31 when we left that hospital room that it would be the last time we would see her on this earth.

I truly believe she is now in a place where there is no pain. A beautiful place, where she can play cards to her heart's content, play golf all the time if she wants, and visit with family and old friends.

I know she would be displeased with me for having written about her. She never liked public display, and never talked about the many things she has accomplished in and for this community.

But even knowing she would be displeased, I wrote anyway.

Friends accept those things about one another. The flaws, the differences, the challenges.

And still they care.

Evie and I are friends.

And I miss her.

Be at peace, my friend, at last."

Unknown to me, I would come to a crossroad that would change my life forever. And bring about one of the most difficult decisions God would ever ask me to make.

Without knowing it, Evie had become my very first experience in dealing with what would become "parish ministry." Meanwhile, God was keeping His eye on me.

CHAPTER EIGHT

As the year of 1994 began, I was wandering aimlessly. Remembering my mother's death and the difficulties I had in accepting it, I vowed not to let that happen again, in attempting to deal with Evie's death. I gave myself permission to grieve. And, as difficult as that may be to comprehend, it truly helped me. Evie's husband had some difficult times, as well, but having watched her pain, he seemed almost relieved for her. Not an overly religious person, he tried to deal with his feelings of loss in his own way. I felt badly for him, because in a matter of two years time he had lost, through death, his father, his wife, his sister and his mother.

Sometimes one person's grief seems insurmountable. For me, I wondered what would become of me. What would I do? It's at these times that our thoughts and prayers—if there are any prayers—are filled with "me" and "mine." I was worried about how I was going to fare, how I was going to live, what I was going to do. Frankly, I felt strongly at this point that God seemed really far away—so distant, in fact, that I could no longer feel His presence. I wanted be able to; I tried reading the Bible, which was something I did little of these days. It just seemed to be a waste of time.

I felt distraught. Nothing seemed to matter any longer. I worked almost mechanically. I did what I did much like a robot. I went through the motions. Things got done, but nothing seemed important any more. Nothing seemed to motivate me in such a way that I felt I was making a difference.

Everything always returned to that original feeling. I just wanted to make a difference, and somehow, now that Evie was gone, it seemed to be more important than ever—and the least likely to ever happen.

I spent endless days and evenings at the cemetery, sometimes talking with Evie. Sometimes just meditating. I wanted to move on, to go on with my life, but I couldn't decide how, and I wasn't certain which way to go.

At length, I finally went to visit with my minister. I went with the idea that I needed to find out what I could do to let it be known in the Iowa Conference that I was available to preach on Sundays when ministers took vacation days. I wanted to expand my world vision—and my income—and I thought this would be a great way to do it.

I went to his office and asked about some way to let people know I was available to speak, and he responded, "You know, there's something here…" he was rifling through the papers on his desk. "That you might be interested in. Let's see……" Then finally, he pulled a piece of paper from the bottom of the pile. "Here it is…take a look at this and see if this is something you might like to do…" Then he left. Left me holding a brochure of some sort.

I was puzzled. I looked at the brochure, then at his back as he disappeared down the hallway to attend a meeting some place else. But, instead of throwing the paper away, I decided to look into it.

I sat in a front pew in the sanctuary and began to read. In Iowa, the Conference of the United Church of Christ had decided to begin a new three-year program to prepare gifted lay persons for Christian Education leadership and to serve as Licensed Lay Ministers. It seemed to be a dream come true for me.

According to the brochure, students would go to classes at the conference office in Des Moines on weekends—one weekend every six weeks. Between classes the students would work on a specific project, returning for the second session of the class, which meant discussing the project—how it was done, what the results were, and what you had gained or learned from the project—and being evaluated by the professor as to what was perceived the value of the project had been.

Through the auspices of the conference office, we would be subjected to the expertise of some of the finest theological seminary professors of the day—talking with us about the Old Testament, the New Testament, preparing the sacraments, preaching, our own spiritual journey, teaching the Scriptures, preparing curriculum for kids and adults, plus a variety of other subjects. It was—and is—called the CENTER/LEARN program, with the CENTER program specifically for qualifying and certifying people as Christian Educators, while the LEARN program specifically for preparing lay persons for the ministry. The CENTER program was for a length of two years; and the LEARN program was for three years. (Actually, the LEARN letters stood for Lay Education for Adults in Religion for the Nineties. Later, when the 90s were concluded, it was changed to stand for Lay Education for Adults in Religion for Now and the Future.)

It seemed a dream come true. The tuition was not outlandish, but I knew I could use some help, especially considering the cost of books. My minister suggested that I talk with the women's fellowship of the church to ask for their financial support. Reluctantly, I did.

Surprisingly, I found that they were very receptive to the idea of having someone pursue a course of study for the ministry, even if it wasn't for the ordained ministry. They offered to pay the tuition, and for every year I was in the program they continued to pay that tuition. An act of love for which I was eternally grateful. It gave them an opportunity to buy into my ministry. They were, after all, a part of my church family, and they were to feel every aspect of my educational process, including the joy of completion and graduation!

The first year began in August, 1994, with the course entitled, "Education: Models, Skills and Theories." Right away I was bewildered. It had been over 30 years since I had been in school, so attempting to recall study skills—as well as my concentration skills—was going to be difficult. I knew it would be taxing. I would need to learn how to do it all over again.

Add to all of this concern about being able to actually learn, the idea that we were really into talking about Christian Education courses and I felt that was NOT my area of expertise. To say I was lost was a bit of an understatement. I wanted to learn, I really did, but it seemed I was way out of my element. I knew something about preparing a sermon, public speaking and the like, but TEACHING? Well, the whole idea was new to me.

For just a second let's backtrack a little. While being associated with the United Methodist church, my sister, Judy, and I were into teaching Sunday school. But I have to admit, she was actually the teacher. I was "along for the ride" or to help with crafts, or discipline the kids. What did I know about actual teaching?

Well, darn it, I was going to find out. I was determined to make it. I was determined to make it—both for my mother, who was still watching over me; and for Evie, who had never stopped.

And so, it began. The courses for the first year were: "Exploring Sacred Scriptures," "Developing Theological and Ethical Perspectives," and "Learning Beyond the Course Book," in addition to the education course. Some of the courses were shared by both first year and second year students, but the program has progressed to the point that now, in the 21st century, the classes are large enough to be independent each year of the study. This speaks well of the entire program.

In the first couple of years, there were as many students from other denominations as there were those with a UCC background. My class totaled seven persons most of the time, more when we shared a class with a different group, but basically, it was five women and two men. All of us were from the UCC denomination, except one, and we referred to him as our "token Presbyterian." We enjoyed a number of laughs together, but at no one's expense; a lot of discussion about our individual faith journeys, and even more discussion about the direction we each felt God was calling us to go.

The second year was exciting for me. The classes were "Organizing Local Church Activities," "Celebrating Worship and the Sacraments," "Preaching" (my favorite), and "Planning for Program and Mission."

For the class dealing with the sacraments, I conducted a survey in my local church discussing the age people should be to begin participating in communion. At the local church, the general belief was that the person needed to be confirmed in the faith first, and that was how I personally believed. Now I was called on to defend that philosophy.

Questions arose about this topic because more and more people were coming into the church membership from other religious backgrounds which permitted communion participation at an earlier age. So, we pondered the question, should parents be allowed to make that decision, or should the church? It was, for me, what the kids call a "no-brainer." The church should decide. No room for discussion—or so I thought. The survey resulted in a number of good arguments for what I perceived to be "the other side," and most of those arguments seemed sound on their own.

Eventually, after a great deal of discussion by Sunday school classes, individuals, lay people as well as clergy, we determined that it should remain as it is. Though we have no objection to parents deciding when their own child should take communion, the church required that confirmation be attained before communion participation would be permitted.

Then came the preaching course…or what I thought would be a "piece of cake."

We conducted what was billed as "A Preach Off," much in the style of the bake-off by the Pillsbury company. We held a contest at a nearby church, with each student preparing a mini-worship service in which they delivered the sermon.

We were free to invite people from our own congregation to sit for the evaluation process. There were several present from the Eldora church on this day. From a hat, we drew our "Scripture for the day," and from that scripture developed a sermon. It was exciting. I knew this was my time to shine.

The "audience" was to complete an evaluation form on each of us, and we would gather and review them at the conclusion of the course, noting each individual gift and areas where improvement could be made. Although I knew I had done well, I was still anxious to hear the words. I had always fought a problem with lack of self-esteem, and these types of evaluations never served a good purpose in my estimation.

My scripture selection was from I Peter 2:2-10, which talked about Christ as the cornerstone, and my sermon was entitled, "Cast in Stone."

Surprise of surprises was that the strongest criticism of my sermon was that it did not have what is called, "inclusive language"—which means I used references to God as male. Several people listed that as distracting on their critique sheets. "Masculine language in reference to God is distracting," said one man. Another person said, "I appreciated the inclusive language scripture but found it very disturbing that God was HE in the sermon." Another commented, "I have gotten used to inclusive language in the pulpit, so I was a little distracted by the masculine pronouns…but you really captured the imagery of the text!"

I had long thought that I was a very inclusive language person. I was really surprised to hear and understand that almost everyone to a person, had noted my references to God as "he." I vowed to work on this a great deal; no one should ever feel left out of God's family, and I knew this subject was important to a number of people, both male and female.

I knew of one person in the Eldora church, for instance, who would never accept any reference to God as a woman. "That's not biblical!" he would say. At the same time, I was aware of a woman in another church who could not accept any reference to God in the masculine form. She believed with all her heart that God is, in fact, a woman.

And that is how each of us comes face-to-face with our God. All are acceptable in God's sight. If we get caught up in all the language differences then there will never be an opportunity for us to learn about or accept God's grace. I will not force my beliefs on someone else, but I have a right to what I believe.

However, being a pastor, a minister of the Word, means that one must be open to all ideas and thoughts about God. Even some that may seem, at first glance, to be totally bizarre. I have come to that point, only after a long and passionate journey in the faith. God guides me.

There were some positive comments on those evaluation sheets, however, which I truly savored. Some of them included:

"Good voice! I love it!" (This comment would come back to haunt me later.)

"Good use of metaphors and illustrations. Right on, Virginia! Very well done."

"Wonderful images. Your message was wonderfully crafted and motivating."

"You brought out some very good points. I had not thought of your text in just this way. You did an excellent job. I would come back to hear you preach again."

"Very good use of voice control and volume."

"Anyone could tune in to your message...well put together."

"You seem very comfortable in leading worship."

"Well done. Strong finish. Excellent use of voice to demonstrate a point."

"I liked your closing with a prayer of dedication. You have a nice voice and use it well."

From an Eldora church member: "Your mother would have been extremely proud of your presentation tonight. We are proud of you, too!" (How much I needed to hear that!)

"I appreciate having scripture read just before the sermon. Holding scripture up to God in thanks, with a line of prayer, and prayer following a sermon, helped me feel 'all is as it should be', Thanks."

"Best overall pulpit presence (leadership). You can tell you've done this for awhile. Great pastoral presence."

That particular congregation went a long way in fueling my ego. When we were finished, everyone else had gone and the professor sat with us to discuss our evaluations. She asked me if I had been nervous. I said, "No." And she said, "I could tell."

When I left for home that Saturday afternoon, I think I was on Cloud No. 9 for sure! It was as if I had received a sign from God that my work as a pulpit supply preacher was affirmed! It was a wonderful feeling.

The third and final year of the educational process included courses in: "Church History," "Parish Assessment and Planning," "Methods of Biblical Interpretation," and "Pastoral Care." In addition to completing the course work, one had also to complete three Pilgrimage retreats, held at Pilgrim Heights, the denominational church camp. I was done, and ready to graduate.

In Iowa each year, the denomination conducts its annual meeting at Grinnell College, a small college located in east central Iowa, which was founded by a group of five congregational ministers in the nineteenth century. A beautiful and tranquil campus, it is easy to see God's handiwork there. A very comfortable and inspiring place to worship the Lord.

It was there, in June of 1997, that three of the original seven graduated. It was a very exhilarating time. It was a time of great achievement.

And so, now what? Life goes on, I knew. But what of me?

It was as though, once again, God was taking care of me— behind the scenes, without my knowledge. I knew I wanted to celebrate this milestone in my life, but I wasn't certain how to go about it. After talking it over with a couple of friends, the church and I decided mutually to have a "service of blessing" in recognition of my completion of the LEARN program in September. And I began to make plans.

In the summer of 1996, I had the opportunity to serve a little country church north of Cedar Falls, called St. Paul's UCC church. They were without a pastor, and needed someone to just do pulpit supply for about six weeks. They offered $125 per week for doing the worship service, and gave no requirements for pastoral care—no hospital or nursing home visits. I took it, and was able to continue working full time at the newspaper while I served there. It was a wonderful, enlightening experience and, though it was a church of the old reformed tradition, I would not have missed that opportunity for the world.

One of the unique things done at the Cedar Falls church was known as "Cookie Sunday." On that Sunday, which was usually the fourth Sunday of the month, everyone brought samples of their favorite cookie and after church served coffee and cookies. Though small, the church had an active Sunday school—even during the summer. They didn't have an active choir during the summer, but they had some beautiful singing voices among them. It was a loving, wonderful experience.

But as for the summer of 1997, I just planned for the special service in September and wondered what was going to happen to me now—what direction God was going to send me. The service was held on September 21, 1997 and it was a delightful celebration unlike any other the church had seen. I was able to share it with family members, church family, and lots of friends. One could feel God's hand in the preparation of this service.

A woman of the church and I sang a duet for this service—it was the last such duet I would ever sing in the Eldora church—but I didn't know it then.

It seemed God was smiling down on the proceedings that afternoon.

But things at the newspaper were not improving. There was a general unrest among my co-workers. No one seemed content with working conditions. Each of us felt we were personally being left out when it came to any decisions involving the operation of the paper.

And I personally was harboring an attitude of feeling that no one cared.

So, I was advised by the conference to attend the North Central Career Development Center in Minneapolis to get some counseling. I felt I was being called to some sort of service to God, but I just couldn't pinpoint it.

The counseling went well; I was told to talk with my employer about some of the issues that were bothering me, and then make my decision. I went home to confront my publisher, only to find that he had no time to discuss it. When we got together to talk almost 30 days later, he listened and seemed to hear. He made some general promises, but basically told me that if I wanted to see change, I needed to do the changing.

Another 30 days passed, and when I could see that nothing, indeed, was going to change…I called the conference office and asked them to find me a church, with a job as pulpit supply—and to do it quickly, before January 1, if possible. I would move, if necessary.

That's when I received a call about a little church in Westside, Iowa.

And a whole new world was opened.

CHAPTER NINE

From 1993 through the winter of 1996-97, I had been involved with covering a total of five murder trials. Residing in a small, rural, Iowa county, it was difficult to believe that the violent crimes of the cities had finally made their way to the rural areas of Iowa.

I didn't want to believe it. One of the murders involved an elderly woman in the county who was reportedly stabbed to death in her bed by a teenager. Stabbed over 60 times. The trial, which lasted a week, and for which the jury deliberated about three hours, was grotesque. I remember as I sat in the courtroom to cover this trial, watching the defendant who was accused of this murder, and wondered what had provoked him to commit this crime. I sat behind the defense table, but caught a glimpse of him just once before he was taken out by one of the deputies.

I remember looking into his dark eyes and feeling extremely cold. In fact, chills went up my spine as I stared into his deep eyes. Then I knew. It was almost as though he were possessed by some demon. I could see the devil in those eyes and I was scared, really scared. I looked away quickly.

Another was a story about a woman motorist, returning to her rural Hardin County home, only to be pulled over by a group of teenagers pretending to have an emergency vehicle. When she did not have any cash for them to take, they shot, beat, and stabbed her to death. Four kids from out-of-state.

The last one involved a young woman who was accused of killing a baby by shaking him to death. Imprisoned, she served a couple of years and then was released for a second trial. Her home was in Eldora. I was completely shocked by this event. I knew this woman, or thought I did. I felt she could never have committed this crime. The trial was long, and the jury took even longer, but reversed the guilty decision. So, we was out of jail at last.

And during those three years, it was my responsibility to provide news stories about these trials, gavel to gavel. It was grueling work. And even though I was able to use a laptop computer to aid in relieving some of the work, it was exhausting. Except for the first trial, all the others were conducted in another courtroom, thinking that the possibility of finding a non-biased jury would be difficult locally.

In most of the cases, except the case involving the woman who was baby-sitting, all of the defendants were teenagers who, because of the violent nature of their acts, were tried as adults.

Autopsy photos were disgusting and horrible to view. As the trials progressed—and took much of my time to cover—I began to lament about how God's children were treating one another. I wondered if this was a trend, or just a passing combination of situations. Surely, it could not continue in this fashion.

Frustrated, it was under this guise that I struggled with

where my chosen profession of journalism was going. I wondered if life truly had no more value than that we had children killing people when things didn't go their way? What had become of God's creation? And, most of all, what was happening to us as God's children? Something was drastically wrong.

It was in this vein that I approached another change in my life.

I was scheduled to meet with the council at the Westside church in early December. I had to change the first interview because I was due to cover the city council meeting, as I had done the first Monday of every month for over thirty years.

I went to Westside a short time later, however, with my credentials in hand.

There is no way for me to explain how I felt when I walked into the room. Never in my life had I felt so welcome.

A variety of questions were asked, both personal and theological. I was worried. I felt somewhat like a fraud. If they asked too many questions, it might be revealed that I was a phony. But, no! I'm not certain who or what was prompting me, but I feel God was guiding my words on that night. When they asked the tough theological questions, the answers were there; my voice spoke clearly and sounded strong, even to me.

We broke for refreshments—coffee and cookies—and then resumed. I was fascinated with their responses to me. It was as though they were welcoming me with open arms. It seemed as though nothing I could say would be taken incorrectly. It was an awesome feeling.

Then we talked contract facts and figures, proceeding through the written contract quickly and purposefully. It went quickly and it went well. I agreed to be there to start the new year with them. I left to begin the two and one-half hour drive home. The woman who was moderator gave me a big hug and said, "I know we'll have a wonderful ministry together."

Accepted. At long last. Accepted for my faith, and in spite of my flaws. How wonderful a feeling it was.

I flew home. I stopped long enough to telephone my sister in Creston and let her know I had accepted the job at Westside, and I would be resigning from the newspaper the next day. She—and I—couldn't believe it.

All the way home, I thought about how I would word the resignation. I was giving him nearly 30 days, and I hoped he would think it was enough. I was excited. My adrenaline was flowing like water. I thought about how he might react, because I knew he was under the impression that I would never leave my post at the newspaper.

So it was important how my resignation was worded.

I remember the letter as though it were yesterday. "I feel that God is asking me to stretch my gifts even more fully in the area of Christian ministry. And, recognizing that no time is a good time for this to happen…I have always said that if the job no longer was fun, I would get out. It has come to that point. You know I have struggled to find some time for myself to do the kind of creative writing I have wanted to do, but that has just not come to fruition."

The people of Westside, however, didn't seem to care that I had conducted only one funeral that I had never done a wedding on my own, or that—except for the time spent at the Cedar Falls church—never worked continuously with the idea of preparing worship on a regular basis each Sunday. They were willing to take a chance with me—even though they knew I was not yet molded by God's hands. It was a church that had made a great leap of faith years earlier when the two churches of the community decided to merge. Two denominations, UCC and

Presbyterian, were melded together to make one. They had been sharing a pastor, now they shared everything. It was a wonderful blend, not without its problems at first, but now those days were in the past.

On January 3, 1998, I came to Westside, brought a few of my "things" with me, and began to settle in. The weather was fairly good, and I struggled with the little television I had purchased to bring to the house. I tried nearly all the outlets, but the machine still wouldn't work!

About the time I was ready to give up, the door bell rang. A couple who are members of the church brought a fresh plant for the parsonage, and luckily the guy owned a hardware store, and offered to help in any way possible. I asked him about the outlets, and he said it probably needed to be hooked up to the cable service. All that made sense, and since I knew nothing about the cable service—and he did—he took care of making all the arrangements so that an hour later, the TV was working! And I was delighted! I had arrived!

Here I was, standing in the center of this old Victorian-style house which serves as the church parsonage, some boxes sitting around, only a few dishes to work with, a microwave and an air-mattress on which to sleep. In the beginning I was going to stay in Westside four days a week, traveling back to Eldora two days a week. I had brought the laptop computer with me, which was compatible with the main computer at home in Eldora and would work with a disk that I could carry back and forth. Everything seemed perfect. I was ready to begin my ministry. Boy, it sounded great to say that.

Great? Here I was, not having met anyone, leaving in Eldora my home, my long-time friends, my profession, and all the people of the church. I wasn't sure if I was going to be able to make it financially; I wasn't even sure if I would make a good minister. I didn't have any assurance that God had really called me to this place. After the couple left, I stood in the middle of the living room, looked around, and wondered, "What have you done? What do you think you are doing here? You're completely out of your element!"

God help me, I prayed. Tell me; show me that I haven't made a mistake in coming here.

I slept unbelievably well that night in a new house and with new surroundings. Having come from a community where a train rarely traveled through, it was an amazing surprise to find I had moved into a community where trains came through on a regular basis. As one parishioner said, "You'll get used to it—they come through about every 15 minutes." I even slept through the sounds of the train whistle. Actually, I found the sound rather soothing.

My first worship service was to be held the next morning and it was to be an installation of new council members. Boy, I was nervous. My hands were clammy and cold and I swear I was shaking in my shoes, though nobody noticed. I tried with everything I had to show that I had everything under control and, after all, hadn't I done this all before?

I had never been this nervous before. For the first time in my life, I uttered a huge prayer skyward before I walked down the aisle toward the pulpit. "God," I whispered, "if this is what you want me to do, send me a sign. Let me know that this is okay with you."

Talk about courage. Talk about a leap of faith. This was it. Nothing I had done in the years before seemed to matter. Everything from this moment on was vital.

Somehow, God gave me the strength to get through that service, though I haven't the slightest idea what I said. I recall that I was installing three people onto the church council that morning, but I couldn't think what I was supposed to call them. It was "elder," but I stumbled over the word, as we went through the service.

We made it through with no serious difficulty. It was a success.

Everyone was kind enough, and I went back to the parsonage to relax for the day. Later that day, it began to snow, sleet and rain. The garage is located behind the house, and by morning, the drive was a solid sheet of ice. I wanted to go exploring through the community, so I was going to take the car from the garage.

I was unaware of how slippery the ice had become, until I pulled out of the garage, turned the wheels to go into the alley behind the house, and then I felt the back wheels go off the edge of the embankment. Westside is constructed on a hill, so the alley had an embankment leading to the neighbor's house. I got out of the car to see how serious it was, and as soon as I removed myself from the car, the car rolled over the embankment into the neighbor's rock garden next door.

I was frustrated as to what to do next. I called a person on the council and asked what to do. She said she would take care of it. I kept checking out the window to see what was going on, only to watch the car sink slowly over the embankment. Soon, a tractor driven by a member of the congregation materialized and it was hooked onto the back bumper, and the car was quickly returned to the garage and safety. Needless to say, it was two days later before I attempt to take the car anywhere!

I had received my sign.

I felt God really wanted me here.

And the feeling continued to grow. The congregation of the Westside church—in fact the people in the community—made me feel welcome from the very start. I wanted with all my heart to succeed here. But only God could make that happen. Only God could honor our ministry together.

It was a slippery start (literally), but somehow I felt we were going to be good together.

When I was being interviewed, I had asked the council how they felt about having a female minister, and nearly everyone said they previously enjoyed a ministry couple and hated to see them go when they left to accept another position. Thank the Lord for their ministry because they paved the way and made it possible for me to come to Westside.

There were issues of healing needed, but people assured me early on that it was not my fault, and I should not worry. We would work through them together. And so we did.

By June, the search committee was becoming frustrated with the idea of trying to find an appropriate candidate for minister. They seemed happy with things as they were. I met with the search committee, and they asked me to see if the conference would consider letting me stay on a permanent basis.

This was unheard of. A person hired for pulpit supply was not supposed to stay at the church they were serving, but we all felt it was right so we asked. We thought it was worth a shot. So, I made an appeal to the conference office. I explained that it seemed to be what both of us wanted, and I asked for them to consider that we were serious about it.

They assured us that they would take it under advisement and, knowing that the conference minister was leaving on vacation soon, they said we would know the answer before she left.

On pins and needles we sat for two days. I received the call first and I was told that it was OK, that I could stay on a permanent basis. Because of the financial stress, I had already decided to move to Westside so that I didn't have to continue paying rent on the apartment in Eldora. Now it was no longer necessary. A month later, a group of people from the congregation went to Eldora, packed up the furniture and moved me to Westside. I was so glad to be here.

After wrestling with my conscience for so long as I attempted to decide what to do with my life, it seemed the determination to go into the ministry of spreading the gospel had not been a mistake. My contract signed, my furniture moved into the parsonage, I was set. Fully aware of the need to be sensitive to everyone's feelings and to serve the entire community of faith, I believed I was ready to do what it took to serve this congregation.

I didn't care what lay ahead. God had called me, not only to the ministry, but to this particular church—that I believed. Little did I know that we both would be tested in a very special way—and very soon. In a way that we could only have imagined.

CHAPTER TEN

Making the transition had not been without its bumps in the road, but no major obstacles prevailed. Acceptance came quickly and easily, for the most part, not only within the church, but throughout the community. Part of the covenant made with the local church was to be visible within the community; and for me that was one of the easiest promises to keep. All my life had been spent being a part of a community. This was just an extension of that.

I had never been so content, so happy in all my life. I breathed a sigh of relief, and relaxed—perhaps for the very first time.

But it seemed it was not to be quiet and calm for long. Things began to change rather rapidly. And it seems life was soon out of control.

An overnight trip to Eldora, and playing five holes of golf left me with a back ache. Saturday, when I stopped to shop on my way home, I found it difficult to get in an out of the car. I knew I would be sore by the time Sunday rolled around.

That turned out to be an understatement. It was late July, 1999, hot and humid, and I could barely get out of bed on that particular Sunday morning. I made it out of bed and into the shower. I was able to get dressed, but I was feeling more and more pain particularly in my right side. I went to the garage and pulled the van out, drove two blocks to a family that I knew would be awake. They were accustomed to arising early to deliver the Sunday newspaper, so I knew I could find help there.

I told them I needed to see a doctor right away. The woman was preparing to take me to the emergency room of the hospital in the next town, and I was giving instructions to the fellow as to what could be done for church services, where the sermon was, and all the information that he would need for that.

I spent a couple of hours in the emergency room, having x-rays taken, a variety of tests, with the final results showing I had some problem with the sciatic nerve on the right side of my spine. They sent me home, although there was no one there to take care of me, and the doctor at the hospital said that if I couldn't manage the pain at home, I was to return and they would consider placing me in the hospital. I went home reluctantly. Members of the church took things in their own hands, put me to bed and called my sister, insisting that she come.

She arrived that Sunday afternoon and began to care for me. However, it was soon very obvious that I could not manage the pain—and we made an appointment to see the doctor on Tuesday.

On Tuesday, we discussed the possibility of entering the hospital for the appropriate care and therapy. The doctor said that many insurance companies won't permit hospital stays without justification, but he would call them to get their approval first.

We waited for what seemed like ages, and then he returned to the exam room. He had gained permission from the insurance company to have me admitted to the hospital, and they would plan a regular regimen of physical therapy, and I could get the much needed rest.

I spent the rest of the week in the hospital, undergoing physical therapy in my room, and waiting for some results. The doctor finally determined that I needed to have an MRI. The machine that contains the MRI only comes to that community on a scheduled basis, so it was planned for Friday afternoon, at whatever time I could be worked in.

Never having had an MRI previously, I was worried. Although I had no tendency toward claustrophobia, I was worried about being able to breathe. I thought it would be too warm inside that chamber and, since I was not supposed to move at all, I figured that would be a problem.

But there were no problems. The close quarters did not bother me, there was a fan of some sort blowing cool air on me, and the people in charge of the test were very careful to let me know how long each segment of the test would take. It want quickly, but I was glad to be out of that tube when it was over!

It would be Monday before any results were known. My sister decided to go home for the weekend, promising to return on Monday.

Results from the MRI showed no pinched nerve, so we continued the scheduled therapy, with people from the congregation transporting me to the city for scheduled appointments. My sister stayed with me for a couple of weeks, until I could do some things for myself, and then she went home, leaving me on my own.

By this time it was August, and the church was making plans for its 25th anniversary as a merged church. We had a committee in place to organize and plan the Sunday event, scheduled for September 19 that year. We had invited former ministers to be a part of the worship that morning, which also included confirmation of three young women. The choir was planning some special music, and everyone had invited family members to return for the celebration. Everything seemed to be falling into place.

Then on September 12, everything fell apart.

I awoke, feeling somewhat out of sorts. I arose, showered, dressed, and sat in the recliner, as the pain became worse. I waited until 7 a.m. on that Sunday morning before calling the same couple once again.

When I reached them, I told them, "I feel a great deal like I did a few weeks ago, except it feels like an elephant is sitting on my chest."

It was all he needed for his mind to send up a red flag. "Do you want me to call the First Responders?" I answered affirmatively, and the paramedics were here in a matter of minutes. In fact, it seemed like seconds.

Much of what followed is vague, at best. I remember having the paramedics give me nitro pills to see how serious the damage was; after they determined that I was in the middle of having a heart attack. One would ask me, "On a scale of one to ten, with one being the worst, how bad is the pain?"

I think I started with, "A four…"

They placed me on a stretcher and wheeled it to the ambulance outside. There were a number of people outside the house as I was taken away, but I don't remember seeing their faces. People were asking questions, wanting to know. But I remember nothing else.

Periodically on the trip to the hospital, one of the paramedics would ask, "On a scale of one to ten, with one being the worst, how bad is the pain?" I think I was able, at one time to say "Six." Basically the pain remained the same. Terrible.

I had no idea who was going to take care of the worship that morning. It was the first day of Sunday school, and a musical group was going to play, so there was no need for a sermon or anything......but I wasn't worried about all of that. Actually, the church never even crossed my mind.

I have little recollection as to what happened next.

Much of it is like a dream.

I remember that there was a new doctor on the scene. I had no idea who he was or what he was doing there.

My conception was that I was placed on a moving cart and taken to a room that was very antiseptic with lots of steel 'furniture.' People in white coats were visiting all around me, whispering so that I couldn't make out what they were saying. They worked over me part of the time, and then conferred together off to the side.

One of the doctors said to me, "We're going to do this angiogram, but we need your signature on this paper first." When I asked the reason, I was told, "If we have to go directly into a bypass operation, we will need your permission to give you blood transfusions."

That seemed reasonable to me, so I signed where I was told.

The next thing I remember is jumbled in my mind. I recall waking—just barely—in a room that looked like it was a waiting room in an airport. It seemed high off the street, with lots of glass windows. I realize now that my imagination was working well overtime, and where these images were coming from I have absolutely no idea.

Many months later, I learned that I had been admitted to the hospital on that first Sunday, my sister was called to come, and 24 hours later I experienced another heart attack. It was then that the doctors decided to send me to Mercy Hospital in Des Moines to the cath lab to see how serious the damage had been.

I remember nothing about this, except I recall the doctor asked me if I wanted to go in a helicopter or by ambulance. I remember saying, "So what's the hurry? Let's just take our time. Go by ambulance." I can see in my mind's eye, the crew placing me in the ambulance and the trip to Des Moines. The crew encouraged me all through the trip. The driver even told me about his own heart surgery. He said, "You'll feel so much better when this is over."

Except for that trip, I recall nothing else.

The room where I awoke, which was a number of weeks later, people seemed to be terribly busy. I knew there were tubes in my nose, and lots of other places. Too many to keep track. I promptly proceeded to remove the feeding tube. No easy task, and very painful.

I was properly reprimanded by the nurse, who told me, "You think it hurt coming out? It's going to hurt much worse going back in…"

Believe me, she was right. But it was my own fault for having taken the thing out in the first place.

Everything from then on is in my memory, though in a fog. I recall having the nurses put in a catheter, only to have me rip it out. Again, I was told that every time it has to be replaced, it gets more painful. And every time it was. I remember pulling it out twice, but it could have been more.

The places where I was located never looked like a hospital room. And there were people all around. I recall that one of the places was like a home, and I was resting on a bed in the basement. It's all very laughable today, but it seemed very real at the time. I had convinced myself that some of the medical personnel had taken me home over the weekend, because the hospital had closed down for the time period.

I watched out the window as cars came and went, loving the movement at night. I recall very vividly that there was a stop-and-go light at the end of the block, and it was great to watch it work.

Funny thing about this? My mind was definitely playing tricks on me, because there were no windows in the room where I was staying!

If all of this sounds crazy, let me be honest and relate to you exactly what was happening at this time. After having an angioplasty, it was determined that I had many blocked arteries—several over 80 percent and two 90 percent or more. The surgeon decided it was necessary to do a heart bypass operation and it needed to be done immediately.

So, on September 15, the surgery was completed, and it was a quintuple by-pass. Surgery was a success. Dr. Grant, the cardiologist, reported to my sister and brother-in-law that all had gone well.

The next day, it was like everything took a backward turn. Dr. Grant came to see my sister and brother-in-law, and he didn't have a smile on his face. He told them that I had had a stroke. My sister told me much later that "it was a long time before we saw him smile again."

Suddenly, I was in critical condition. For five days I was considered near death. And as I was to learn much later, the people of Westside, Arcadia and Vail, were praying pretty hard for me to get better. Not just to survive, but get better. It would be a contributing factor to keep me on the road to recovery.

I was in intensive care. Though I was almost conscious, I was not entirely aware of what was going on. People came into my room and made me do some unbelievable stuff. Like reaching across my body with the left hand. It took me some time to realize my left arm was paralyzed, which is what made these exercises necessary.

I do recall one time in the middle of these exercises, becoming incredibly tired. I just stopped, and asked the therapist, "Do we have to continue?" When she said, "Yes," I knew I was doomed. They were very demanding, or so it seemed to me. They stretched me beyond my limit. I couldn't believe some of the things they were asking me to do.

Most of the stuff we were doing in the early days of my recovery, after it was determined that I was, indeed, going to survive, are lost in my memory. My sister has more details stored in her memory than I. What I do remember was confusing enough.

I remember traveling several miles to a place which was supposed to help in the recovery. (This actually did not happen.) But it made me feel as though I were making some progress.

I actually spent four weeks in intensive care. At the end of that time, I remember my sister visiting me and telling me that the next time she came, she hoped that I had been moved to a room with a view. In intensive care, there were no windows.

When she returned, I was happy to tell her that I finally was going to be moved to a room with a view. She was delighted as well.

I should explain at this point that the doctors and nurses knew that a great deal of rehabilitation was called for in the next several weeks. I had lost motor control in my legs and my arms, and my ability to talk was questionable. A trachea was placed in my throat, and breathing exercises were conducted on a daily basis.

I thought the person doing the breathing exercises was a Methodist church official in the state of Iowa. I talked to her about a number of ways our two denominations could work together. As I think about it now, I wonder what planet she thought I had come from. All those conversations were ridiculous.

Important for you to remember at this point was that very few people could understand a word I was saying; communicating was nearly impossible. People from the church would come to visit and, try as I would, I could not make them understand me. People from the conference office would come to visit, and, try as I would, I could not make them understand me. People from my former home, Eldora, would come to visit and, try as I would, I could not make them understand me. It was the most frustrating effort of my life.

Many nights I cried myself to sleep. I'm not certain if the nurses were aware of it or not, but I did it anyway.

I was worried. Worried about what was going to happen to me. How I was going to live. Where I was going to live? I had no idea whether or not I was ever going to be able to preach—or write—again. I prayed to God, asking, "Why?" I wanted to know why God had brought me to this marvelous place, let me do what I felt was my life-long desire, and then tore me away – before I ever had a chance to get started. I didn't even know if I would be able to walk again, to talk again normally, to feed myself or dress myself or take a shower!

I was angry, and full of questions. And, yes, for a while, I was angry at God. I pounded the pillows several nights. I was afraid of what was ahead. I didn't know if I could do what I had to do to survive and improve.

What began after I was removed from intensive care amounted to an intense therapy effort, going to a lower floor where there was a "gym" or exercise room where patients were put through their paces. I became acquainted with four or five other patients who were dealing with a variety of ailments but trying to strengthen their muscles for one reason or another. Most were in what seemed to be worse shape than I.

One was learning to walk with an artificial limb. Another was recovering from a back injury. We would work intensely twice a day with a break in between for lunch and a short nap before taking up the effort again. There was physical therapy, occupational therapy, speech therapy, and a battery of tests to evaluate my thinking skills.

It was a grueling schedule—for the nurses and therapists as well as myself—and at one point, I gave up. When the aide came to my room to get me, I refused to go. She was small enough; she wasn't going to make me. So, I got away with it that time. I told her I was tired from the effort in the morning and wouldn't go. I knew I better not try it again.

Then I graduated to the parallel bars and walking with help, I knew I was on the way to recovery. People from the church came to watch on one occasion, and one day a fellow from Eldora came to see how I was getting along. It felt great to show them what I could do.

I knew I had to reach a certain point before I would graduate to the next step, which was just short of an assisted living situation, but I still had some difficulty dealing with the food. It was usually in a pureed state and not very tasty, in fact, no taste at all.

In the fall of 1998, I had been diagnosed with diabetes, so each night at different intervals; the nurse would come into my room and take a sample of blood to check the level of my blood sugar. A variety of medications were tried before we found something that seemed to work.

So the medical personnel were working with several things at once: a person recovering from heart by-pass surgery, a person recovering from a stroke, and a person with diabetes and high blood pressure.

But, I was determined to one day return home and to walk on my own two feet. And I was determined to walk once again down the aisle of the church, to stand at the pulpit to preach again, and to do it without a walker, crutches, cane or any other device!

People who came from the church told me not to worry about any of it, that they would be willing to have me preach while sitting in a chair in the sanctuary; they didn't care.

Well, maybe they didn't. But I did. And I was determined to make this work.

CHAPTER ELEVEN

Work continued on the rehabilitation effort. At times, I felt I was getting nowhere. Other times we rejoiced with each achievement, no matter how small.

Standing from a sitting position became a reason to celebrate. Walking with the aid of a walker was another. Getting through the battery of tests and exercises in an attempt to strengthen my left arm and leg was yet another. For weeks this routine went on.

If I told you I was a kind and considerate patient, I would be lying. I was a terrible patient. I ripped out the feeding tubes, the catheter and, finally removed the trachea—several times. After I first had the stroke, I had to be physically restrained. They said it was to protect myself, and I'm certain that was right. It was also to stop me from tearing out the tubes!

I think back on that experience and can't believe how difficult I must have been as a patient. No one ever complained, that I know of, but I knew what I was doing wasn't right.

Women of the church came to visit me and I grilled them

with questions about things that were going on in the church. It was difficult to make them understand me, but I kept trying.

I wanted someone from the church to bring my laptop computer to the hospital, because I just knew that if I could work on the computer, I would be able to do some creative writing and rebuild my self-esteem. I really thought at this point that is what I needed to do.

They were kind. They humored me. They assured me that they would see to it that I got the laptop, and that day my ego grew at least three sizes. I had no idea if I could do it; I would struggle with my creativity for months, but at least for the time being, I felt encouraged. It seemed possible that I had not lost everything. But there was still a long way to go. I had to know.

Finally, a cover was placed on the trachea to make it possible for me to speak, but it was unsuccessful. I kept struggling with some speech problems, but nothing seemed to help. It was as though everyone thought that everything else needed to be fixed first, and then we would work on the voice.

One of the therapists who worked with me on a regular basis found she liked my voice during the brief period of time when the cap on the trachea worked. She said, "You have a nice voice. I've never heard it before. It's lovely." That was the first time anyone ever said that to me. And oh, how I longed to hear it.

The next best thing seemed to be a white board, with felt tip pens. I could write my messages, and that way I wouldn't have to talk. No matter that I wasn't using my vocal chords. We would worry about that later. If anyone came to visit, I would try writing my messages to them, and that seemed to work. It really helped communications.

After five weeks, I was placed on a different floor, and encouraged to be more independent. At this time in my hospital stay, I was told to get out of bed on a daily basis and dress each day. I was to take a shower on a daily basis, which for me, meant to wash my hair, and I was to do some exercises on my own, other than what was being done in therapy.

The work continued. I learned to button clothes using a special apron in therapy. The same for using zippers and snaps. It was as though my mother were teaching me these things all over again. Learning to tie my shoes as a child was never a "snap" for me, so imagine what it was like going through the process over again.

It was truly an education. It was while I was in this independent living place that I received my first solid food, and did it taste good! It took a while to get used to solid food again. It seemed strange.

This sounds really crazy, but at first I was required to take a shower with someone in the room with me, just in case I would fall. And, at first, I needed to have a chair in the shower, because I was not steady enough to stand for any length of time.

I still needed to have help getting to the bathroom, and it was a cause for celebration the day I was told that I could try it on my own! I never would have believed that I could be so excited about the idea of going to the bathroom by myself.

Everything I did, brushing my teeth, combing my hair, putting on my shoes—everything—became a major learning task. Going to dinner and sitting at a regular table, having a conversation with those around me, was a special treat. While I had some weakness on the left side of my face, I did not experience some of the excessive drooling usually associated with someone who has had a stroke.

Having my first dish of ice cream was delightful, and there is no way to tell you how excited I was when I was able to take a shower, standing the entire time, by myself!

At long last, I felt there was a light at the end of the tunnel. I was going to make it. There might me a few flaws, a few difficulties which might hold be back, but I knew I would make it. My laptop showed up from home, and I asked the nurses to hook it up for me. It needed to be charged for power.

I waited. Then I tried to type. But it was as if I didn't know how. My fingers were clumsy and unable to create the words I needed. The letters were all jumbled. Nothing coherent showed up on the screen. I sat there for a minute, and then just sobbed uncontrollably. It seemed as though my dreams were dashed. I wanted to give up. I didn't want to try anymore.

And most certainly I did not want to pray about it. I was convinced that God was tired of hearing my pleas. At that moment, God seemed very, very far away. Oh, I knew that wasn't the case, but right then I didn't care. I was feeling extremely sorry for myself.

And, unfortunately, right at the moment some friends from high school stopped to visit, and all they got from me were a bunch of complaints. At one point, I threw the white board on which I was writing, along with the pen, across the room. There was no denying my anger.

At various times during my hospitalization, the staff would have evaluation sessions about me. Each of the departments— speech, physical therapy, and occupational therapy—would discuss whether or not I was making progress and if I was ready for the next level of the process.

Over several weeks, there had been a couple of times when I had fallen. Once occurred in the exercise room, another in the hospital room, and once when I had gotten out of the shower. In all instances, my left knee had just given way. There was nothing I could do to control it.

At last they began to talk about sending me back to the

Carroll hospital. I was delighted, but there was one final meeting of the staff before I could get permission to go. I was called into the room to meet with them.

The speech therapist was a little reluctant to release me; she said it might be too soon. The others seemed willing to let me try being on my own, and I wanted to cheer.

But I knew there was still work to be done. Making a promise was one thing. Seeing it through was another.

My sister seemed equally as concerned about my recovery not stopping. Before I could be returned to the Carroll hospital, she wanted to be reassured that the hospital had a qualified speech therapist so that she could be sure my progress would continue.

At this point, my speech was coherent, but it sounded more like "mush." And, at times, I seemed confused. Although I didn't want to ever admit that, I knew that my thoughts sometimes went wandering, and I couldn't sit to think long enough to put a couple of sentences together. Try as I might.

But their fears quickly disappeared when they met the speech therapist and found her to be more than adequate. She was to meet with me when I returned to the local hospital and begin with a couple of aptitude tests so that she could see where I was in the process.

The first day we met, she put me through a couple of quick tests, one of which amounted to drawing a clock and telling her—through drawing a picture showing what time it was. I failed miserably, but I didn't know it then. She didn't let me see the clock I had drawn until she felt I was ready – which was, thankfully, sometime later.

The other test was in the form of a puzzle. I couldn't solve it, no matter how I tried. Then there was a series of questions— many of them trick questions—to try my thinking skills. I failed at that as well.

She came each day, gave me more tests, and left some sheets of games, puzzles and brain teasers for me to work on between visits.

There began to be some talk about going home, but first, a visit from the doctor. He wanted to know about the house—if everything I needed was on the main floor. I assured him that it was, except the garage. There was no discussion about when I would be able to drive again, and I didn't push it.

My heart leaped into my throat—could it be? Would I finally get the chance to go home? The doctor said, "Now, now wait a minute. All the therapists have to agree or it won't happen. They will meet on Friday morning to discuss your case and then decide. If you don't go on Friday, we won't talk about it again until Monday."

I really wanted this to happen, but I didn't know if I was ready. My sister had been with me since I returned from Des Moines, but now she decided to go home, and then come back on Friday, planning to take me home and stay for a while. She was certain that would help the doctor to make his decision about sending me home. It sounded really good, but would it be possible?

On Friday morning, I met with the speech therapist one more time. For one more test. It was an oral test that she kept score for me as we went along. It was a higher level of test than she usually used on stroke patients. When we were done, she had taken away some points on a question that I had answered, calling for me to name animals that started with the letter 'B', because I reacted too slowly. She commented, "I just can't give you 100 percent, but you did very, very well. By the way, I have never given anyone a 100." And then she showed me the picture of the clock I had drawn on that first day. It was supposed to show the time as 6:30, but it looked more like a barometer than a clock.

The therapists met as planned. A schedule was set for me to return to the hospital on a regular basis for physical and occupational therapy, but the speech therapist gave her permission for me to be released.

The day was October 29, 1999.

And I was going home. Just over eight weeks after I'd had the first heart attack.

My sister took me home, bag and baggage, and we were met at the house by the same couple who greeted me on the first day I came to Westside. He was putting a hand bar in the bathroom to make it easier for me to rise from the toilet; otherwise the house was ready for me.

The next day, my sister and I sat at the kitchen table and talked. She came prepared to stay as long as three weeks, which would take us through Thanksgiving that year. We got paper and pencil, and as we sat there, we talked about what I would have to be able to do in able for her to go home. We made a list.

On that list were a variety of things including, making my bed by myself; getting to the church by myself; handling the stairs by myself; and so on. And we started to work.

The following Monday night, the church council met. After the meeting the secretary came to the house to give me a report. She said, "I have two things to tell you. First of all, you need to get well. And you need to take whatever time it takes to do that. Second, you have a job here as long as you want it." It was just what I wanted to hear.

But, no one from the church had heard me preach yet. No one from the church even knew if I could preach again! What a great leap of faith for them! I didn't even know if I could preach again.

In the process of working through therapy, I called the worship committee together to talk about what plans had been made for filling the pulpit for the rest of the month. Everything seemed to be in place until the last Sunday in November, which happened to be the first Sunday in Advent.

Several churches in the area join together to sponsor an ecumenical Thanksgiving service, alternating locations each year. It was our turn to host the service in 1999, and everything was in place for it—I just had to work on the program, and assign duties to other members of the clergy. So, I told the worship committee that I would set a goal of returning to the pulpit on November 28, the first Sunday of Advent.

Though a few people questioned if I was returning to the pulpit too soon, everyone agreed that I needed to try it. In the meantime, my sister kept after me to begin working on my first sermon. I was afraid. What if I couldn't do it? What if I was no longer able to be creative? What if?

I felt my whole life was wrapped in that one sermon.

The ecumenical service was held the week before my first sermon, and, as host church, I offered the words of welcome to the joint congregation. As I did so…the crowd began to stand and applaud. And they continued until the entire group was applauding.

November 28 came and went, and I was a big hit from the pulpit. Everyone seemed glad to have me back. And, God knows, I was very happy to be back. It was halting and I stumbled over the words. I skipped over a couple of things in the bulletin.

I believed that, for some reason, by life had been spared. God pulled me from the "depths of death," but for what reason was a puzzle to me. For many months, as I worked through therapy and continued to deal with climbing stairs and other small difficulties, I wondered. "If my life was spared for a reason," I would ask, "what could that reason be?"

Once again, my faith was being tested.

It took a long time for me to realize it, but I do understand now that the reason for which I was spared was very simple. The job for which I was saved was obvious—to preach the word of God in the United Church at Westside. And, knowing that, I was doing what God wanted me to do.

I thought about others who have wondered at times what God's plan is for them, how they struggled with that concept.

God didn't want me to start with people of Westside, and then call me away, God gave me the sign I had asked for so many months before. God wanted me here, and that was the message I received from the people of Westside—now I knew they wanted me here, too.

And what better way to send the message of God's love?

There's no way to express in words how valuable the prayers of the people were for me that year—and have remained since that time.

God is good.

In the days and weeks that followed, I continued physical therapy to strengthen my leg muscles. I walked with a walker first, then switched to a cane. In the church are two steps leading to the altar. I wanted to get to the point that I did not need to use a cane to get up those steps. I asked a couple of people from the congregation, if a handrail might be placed on the right side, so that I could get to the pulpit more easily. I asked, and it was provided.

I had been told when I returned home that November, that the people didn't care if I had to sit in a wheel chair to preach, they still wanted me to preach. I didn't want to do that, but it set me to thinking. My dining room set has four captain's chairs, so

I had my sister take one of them to the sanctuary, setting it behind the pulpit. The reason I selected one of these chairs was because they had arms, and using these arms made it easier for me to rise from a sitting position.

During this time, it was not unusual for me to burst into tears at a drop of a hat. Someone would say something about how lucky I had been, or how wonderful it was that I was able to "come back", and I would be sobbing uncontrollably. No special reason. It would happen whether it was a seven year old child talking with me, or an 80-year-old. I was extremely emotional during the next two years, while I was still in therapy, and recovering from all that had happened to me.

I remember sharing with my sister, my fear of the future. What if it (heart attack) happened again? What if, that time, I didn't make it? She assured me that "things have been fixed; there should be no problems now. It's like starting new!"

Eventually, the chair came back home, on the Sunday after Easter, 2002. The handrail is still there, but used rarely.

I still can burst into tears in an instant, but it's not quite as emotional as it was. It has taken a long time to come through this experience. I still have a weakness on my left side from the stroke, and have some troubles with stairs, for which I still use a cane, but overall, I have learned to cope with the entire situation. It is so much better now than when I first began rehab. I thought a lot of my life had been lost.

CHAPTER TWELVE

Thankfully, and gratefully, my life goes on. I am convinced that only through the grace of God and the prayers of the people who have been a part of my life, I am here doing God's work in my communities.

God IS good. I will never question that, or question God's purpose for my life again.

Once you have learned to trust completely in God and accept God's unconditional love, you know that things will work together for good.

Not much later and my faith – and the church's – was tested once again. I had come through the surgery and recovered nearly completely from the stroke, but during the years 2001-2003, I was having difficulty getting caught up with the medical bills which resulted from those devastating times.

I could see that I was going to have to do something with my cash flow in order to improve it. My car was getting worn, and since I need my car for the work that I do, I needed to look seriously at trading it for a different model. When it comes time for me to make decisions about situations such as this, I usually sit and make a list of all the pros and cons of the proposal, then decide whether or not I can afford it. I searched all the local car dealers to see what sort of deals they had available and found that I could buy a 2001 car for about $12,000 with very little mileage on it.

Well, this is one of those instances where I pushed the pencil to see if it would all work. I decided it would, if I kept very close watch on my funds each month. There would be very little money left for clothes or other necessities, but I would have to work around that. So, in January 2004, I decided to go ahead and purchase it.

I didn't know it then, of course, but that was the beginning of the end. Although I attempted to watch my funding rather closely, it was difficult, and I found myself losing ground. I don't usually have many people to buy presents for at Christmas time, but I told my family not to expect anything from me for Christmas, 2004. If the situation changed, I would let them know.

Although it was difficult to face, it appeared as though I was going to have to declare bankruptcy before the end of the year even though it was something I dreaded doing. The soul searching began seriously about October 1 and became more intense as the months rolled by.

In 2003, an attorney friend said he would look into trying to find out what went wrong with the medical bills so that I found myself in this position. We now have a cardboard box filled with emails, letters and copies of bills with no concrete evidence that could be used in filing a legitimate law suit against the insurance company, or any of the medical providers. The main problem seemed to come with the cost charged by the hospital where I had the surgery and where I was treated for the stroke following the surgery – in the room charges.

The insurance, which is purchased through the church, just didn't seem to me to be doing what it had promised in the beginning when I first went into ministry. Even though others tried to tell me differently, I knew that the only one to really be blamed for my financial situation was me.

When my friend and I had explored about all we could on our own, we went to church officials in Des Moines, to see if they would support us if we decided to file a suit with the insurance carrier. After much discussion, the message we received from those officials was that, if we did that, we would be on our own.

As we left the office in Des Moines, my friend told me that the decision was up to me. He would pursue whatever course of action I decided was necessary. He was doing all of this work "pro bono" or free, as a part of our friendship.

It took me several days to come to a decision. When I sent that last email message to my friend, I told him that I felt it wasn't worth the fight, since we had no hard evidence – nothing on paper that would prove our case. I thanked him profusely for his help, but I asked him to stop the process.

It took several weeks of soul-searching once again for me to come to the conclusion that I really had no choice. I would have to proceed with the bankruptcy process.

I searched for an attorney to begin the process, and went several different directions before coming to the conclusion that I couldn't even afford a bankruptcy attorney. One attorney that I called said his cost would be $650, and the cost of filing would be $210, and as soon as I sent him that check, he would begin the paper work. When I thought about the fact that I didn't have $860, I thought better of pursuing it that way.

Then I found out about a firm online that would provide help for you to fill out all the paperwork on your own and submit the document without the benefit of an attorney.

I sent for the packet of information and began to prepare the paperwork. I knew I had to file the papers in federal court in Sioux City, so late on the afternoon of December 29, 2004; I made the trip and filed the documents in bankruptcy court. The drive back to Westside was the longest in my life. Over the years in dealing with my alcoholism, I have been tempted to jump (or fall) off the wagon, but something always stopped me before I made that plunge.

On this particular day, I was feeling as much like a failure as anyone could, so I pulled off the interstate, drove into a town that had several particularly sad looking bars, and parked in front of one of them. When I reached the city of Onawa, which is about half way between Westside and Sioux City, I felt as though I had sunk about as low as I could with my life.

I pulled up and parked in front of a bar, stared at the door, with its lighted signs, and enticing entrance. I had convinced myself it was time for a drink. I was ready to start drinking again. I was almost desperate to start drinking again. I started to get out of the car, walked up to the door, put my hand on the handle, and then stopped suddenly.

On other occasions when this has happened to me, I have always been able to snap out of it by remembering all the damage I had brought on people's lives in the past. Now, 30 years after taking my last drink, I wasn't so sure whether or not I wanted to start again. I took a walk down the street, looking in store windows, and then crossed the street and did the same thing on the other side. I told myself that I deserved something for enduring my first appearance in bankruptcy court, and one drink wouldn't hurt anyone.

But I knew that story, too, wouldn't hold water.

Finally, knowing I really couldn't afford the price of a drink, I turned toward my car and started the rest of the trip home. I wanted a drink, but I hadn't taken it.

Later, I would be proud of that action. But for now, I just felt really, really, low. That feeling stayed with me for the next several months as I made three more trips to Sioux City and the federal bankruptcy court. The rules for bankruptcy would be changed later in 2005, making it more difficult for someone like me to file bankruptcy.

It took about five months to go through all the necessary hoops. Not hiring an attorney to oversee the case was probably a mistake. I lost my personal life insurance policy, because I didn't know that it was not exempt. And, of course, an attorney would have known that.

Several months after the debt was discharged by the court, I continued to think that, someday, someway, I will attempt to pay those creditors back who tried to help me in any way. My sister and brother-in-law tried to help me out, and I swore that I would pay them back – someday.

I told only about six of my closest friends that I had done this. I knew it could be printed in the Sioux City Journal, but I took the chance, that no one in our area paid that much attention to those lists. That, too, was wrong. It appeared in the Sioux City paper, and then the list was spread among area lenders and appraisers. Soon, the word was out. Because some of the people in the congregation showed some concern, I met privately with each of them to explain the reason for my decision.

All of that seemed to go very well, and most of the people with whom I talked said they understood. However, I wasn't so sure.

Although it was something I never spoke with the people in general about, I did make an announcement at the regular meeting of the church council. Their reaction was pretty much non-committal. I told them I accepted all the responsibility for the conditions surrounding this decision. Basically, I have no idea, with the exception of a few individuals, how it has been received by the congregation and the community as a whole. For some people, they found that not talking about it would make the whole subject go away. And, perhaps that is the right approach.

Since this has transpired, the denomination has changed its insurance carrier, and I have learned of others ministers in the area (not of the same denomination) who have had to declare bankruptcy due to the high cost of medical expenses these days.

I kept thinking of those old clichés that people come up with at times such as these: "It'll be alright. This, too, will pass."

But one thing I do know: if the things that come to us don't kill us, they make us stronger. At least I hope that is the case.

My personal spiritual journey has brought me a long way – on trails that I never would have imagined. Originally, my dream had been to be a journalist, and that was fulfilled. I had no fantasy about serving as a parish minister, but even that has been fulfilled. I am into my eighth year with the congregation at Westside, with no idea of where the future path will take me., but I am ready for the trip, thanks to all that God has provided. As well as the friends I have acquired along the way.

The journey is far from over. It has barely begun. But it has been an exciting and sometimes scary journey. The important thing to remember is to be open to where God leads you on this journey. Be ready to try something new, regardless of whether or not you think it is something you can do.

God knows you better than you know yourself. Remember? He's the one who knows even your name! And, with God, nothing is impossible. You will be surprised at what you can do, with God's help. God can do what you cannot do alone.

I have often wondered how people who have no faith mange to cope. I know that, without it, I never would have made it this far. I would either have died at the bottom of a whiskey bottle, or in the hospital after that first heart attack.

But, with God guiding me, and a large faith community for support, there was no way I could lose, in any of these trials. Having completed this book has been a dream of mine that I have long held. All I ever wanted to do was make a difference in someone's life. I hope this has accomplished that. I am reminded of something that I continually tell my confirmation students, "Always keep sight of your dreams."

I thank God that I am a woman of faith, and that I know in my heart God is my constant companion. Praise God!